BACK RC
OF THE
CATALAN
PYRENEES
CARDONA TO
EL PONT DE SUERT
Duncan Gough

Chie, lots of love Clive X

"Travel isn't always pretty. It isn't always comfortable. Sometimes it hurts, it even breaks your heart. But that's okay. The journey changes you; it should change you. It leaves marks on your memory, on your consciousness, on your heart, and on your body. You take something with you. Hopefully, you leave something good behind."

Anthony Bourdain

Enquiries concerning reproduction outside those terms should be sent to the publishers:

HOMBRE

Bronheulog, Fronfraith Lane, Comins Coch, Aberystwyth, Ceredigion, SY23 3BE, Wales.

Tel: 01970 625580

Email: duncangough001@gmail.com

Web: www.duncan-spanish-travel.com

ISBN 978-0-9957454-6-3

British Library Cataloguing in Publication Data.

A catalogue record for this book is available from the British Library.

Printed and bound by

ZENITH MEDIA
PART OF ZENITH PRINT GROUP

Typeset in Segue UI 12pt by Hombre
First Edition 2020

HOMBRE

CONTENTS

Ways of travelling

It is easy to let one's travels and travelling become destination orientated. Naturally one is likely to start with a list of places you think it would be interesting to visit, you'll look for nice roads to get there but the focus all too easily drifts into a fixation with ticking off the points of the itinerary. This is putting you in the world, a sense of achievement being related to your standing at this spot having ridden that road in this much time.

Can you turn it around? Can you say; does anyone here care that I am here? Have I actually related to those who live their lives here? Have I achieved even the most basic understanding of the country I am in?

I have always worked for at least a cursory knowledge, from Zululand to Sweden and Greece to Ireland, and all the places in between that I have ended up.

I prefer to have an outline of a trip but am happy to change it on a whim or happenstance. I also concentrate on being a sponge and soaking up all the experiences offered me. A few brief words to a waiter, waitress or a local about the weather or how pretty the village is enrich both of our experiences of the day. I must admit it is easier when travelling solo but when with a group a little bit of effort to widen your interactions can really pay off.

I am always looking for clues to how a different culture and society works, looking and listening for the keys to local behaviour. Whether it is Africa, Europe or elsewhere there are always things to pick up on.

If you say *gracias* (thank you), which you should for a door opening or a seat in a bar, you will often get *por nada* or *de nada* (for nothing) as a response, reinforcing their pleasure in doing you a service. So, use these responses yourself.

In some lands people make a small bow or other gesture on meeting and greeting, in others a handshake is not normal or wanted. In Iberia the double-cheek kiss with women is common in many situations; a shoulder clasp or double handshake with men (particularly by the second or third time you meet). Iberia is a very tactile and open society.

Architecture often gives clues to the way people live now, and in the past: from the 'Arabic' inner courtyards of Andalusia to the way in which many shops are on the ground floor of apartment buildings in Iberian towns, the resulting integration of populace and business perhaps accounting for the great number of little family-run shops.

Fiestas and Saints Days, even the controversial bullfighting or bull running, are all part of the colour and texture of Iberia. You never know when you are going to be able to be included in one of these events. Take the plunge when invited and give yourself to the experience without criticism or judgement until you understand at least something of the importance for the people involved. Can you imagine what they would make of fox hunting? Chasing an animal to death and not giving it a chance of fighting back? But there are people who say it is part of our heritage. Allow others their heritage and then question WHY? With yours and theirs.

Fiesta parades whether religious or 'moros y christianos' and other folk events are an integral part of the social fabric; the bands that play and the *filas* 'clubs' that take part spend all year meeting and rehearsing, building costumes or floats. They are always across generations and social standing.

By making these things a true part of your experience, you bring the world into you and are richer for it.

Me, I'll talk to anyone, even a *burro*! Actually he was quite lonely and was appreciative.

Route overview

This book completes my 'grand tour' of the Catalan Pyrenees bringing us back to El Pont de Suert where we started in Book 1. The route in this book (red on the map opposite) takes us from Cardona to El Pont de Suert via Vielha with a few detours in between covering around 440 km or 270 miles. They include parts of *Moturisme* (see page 75) routes 1,2,3,8 and 9 which are downloadable from their website.

Place names can be spelled differently on directional road signs so where possible when describing part of a route I use the version on the signpost at that location. It is also useful to try and understand a little of the pronunciation in case you want to ask your way (more interactive than fiddling with your phone/satnav) or are responding to a query about needing help. In Spanish vowels do <u>not</u> change their sound depending who is leaning on them, so for instance the 'o' in Cardona is the same as the 'o' in on. So please think about how you pronounce Potes in the Picos! Some consonants are sounded differently from the English particularly J, H and V. With 'J' I always think of the way in which the name Jesus is pronounced in Spanish: "Heysoos". Jaca is "haka". The 'H' is barely sounded (an expiration) so *hola* is more like "olla". 'V' is a soft 'B'. Vielha is "beeaya". I find that two 'L's' always need a moment's thought, coming from Wales where they are slurred together because in Spanish they are like a 'Y'. So Ripoll is "Ripoy" and Lleida is "Ye-ida".

Catalan and Valenciana and other regional dialects do vary from the standard Castilian so do listen to the way things are said around you.

The petrol stations at Cardona are a little out of the way (see map opposite). There are four in Berga but they are not that easy to find, so it is 55 miles to the easy one at Ripoll if doing that part of the route.

The detour to Ripoll was a direct result of reading my Michelin 1:400,000 map and noticing the number of bends on the way to the town. The detour to Gósol because I knew a good place to stay and to follow up on details from the 'Route of the Cathars' that I found at the Santuari de Queralt above Berga. Exploring La Pobla de Lillet and Castellar de n'Hug was a desire to find a way round the 'expensive' Tunel de Cadí.

On pages 32-35 there are suggestions for some off-road exploration though I have not completed all of them.

The Catalan Pyrenees

FRANCE

ANDORRA

VIELHA

N-230

C-28

ANDORRA LA VELLA

LAVORSI

C-13

EL PONT DE SUERT

SORT

PUIGCERDA

N-260

RIBES DE FRESER

N-230

N-260

SENTERADA

N-260

N-260

LA SEU D'URGELL

N-145

N-260

BELVER DE CERDANYA

N-260

N-260

C-16

BAGÀ

CAMPDEVAOL

N-26

ARAGON

N-230

N-260

C-13

LA POBLA DE SEGUR

C-14

TUIXENT

GOSÓL

LA POBLA DE LILLET

C-26

TREMP

N-230

ORGANYA

OLIANA

SANT LLORENÇ DE MORUNYS

RIPOLL

C-17

ISONA

C-14

C-26

BERGA

ÀGER

C-13

BASSELLA

SOLSONA

NAVEIS

C-26

C-16

VIC

CAMARASA

PONTS

CARDONA

C-25

ARTESA DE SEGRE

EL MIRACLE

C-55

CUBELLS

GUISSONA

C-26

BALAGUER

C-13

C-25

MANRESA

C-55

A-2

CERVERA

C-16

LLEIDA

TÀRREGA

CATALONIA

MONTSERRAT

BARCELONA

Back Roads to the Catalan Pyrenees - Biscay ports to El Pont de Suert (0)
Back Roads of the Catalan Pyrenees - El Pont de Suert to La Seu d'Urgell (1)
Back Roads of the Catalan Pyrenees - La Seu d'Urgell to Solsona (2)
Back Roads of the Catalan Pyrenees - Solsona to Cardona (3)
Back Roads of the Catalan Pyrenees - Cardona to El Pont de Suert (4)

The map above shows the routes (and detours) that are covered in the Catalan Pyrenees series of 4 books. Book (0) arrives at El Pont de Suert from the Biscay Ports. The whole tour is a little over 1,000 km or around 620 miles, depending on how many of my detours you take.

8 - CARDONA TO EL PONT DE SUERT

Cardona

Cardona is covered in greater detail at the end of Book 3 in the series, Solsona to Cardona.

This is a spectacular place to visit with the medieval castle dominating the town from its perch on the rocky spur created by a curve of the river Cardener. The castle is one of the most important in the whole of Spain and was originally built by Wilfred the Hairy in 886. There has of course been quite a lot of rebuilding over the years and it is now predominantly Romanesque and Gothic in style. Probably the oldest significant structure is the Torre de la Minyona an 11th-century tower 15 metres high. The 'Tower of the Girl' refers to an 18th-century legend about the hopeless love between the daughter of the Viscount and a Muslim leader; it is said that she was locked in the tower where she died of a broken heart.

Salt has been the wealth and might of Cardona for centuries and has been mined here since Roman times. Some of the rock is transparent and has been used for carving by local artists. 'The Salt Mountain' is a unique natural deposit which is actually a giant pothole caused by rainwater eroding the rock salt. The accessible top part goes down 120 mts but other bits extend to a depth of two kilometres. A fascinating guided tour takes about an hour.

There is a Parador in the castle, which is a superb place to stay. One can then wander down into the town and explore the narrow alleyways and small *plaças*, little bars and interesting shops tucked away underneath flats and apartments: a typical Iberian town.

Cardona castle

Cardona to Berga

Both routes are around 50 km (30 miles) and can take an hour or more, if you stop on the way.

The main C-55 road runs between Solsona and Manresa and loops around Cardona close to the El Cardener river. We are going to head towards Solsona on it for 10 km before turning off onto the back roads that will take us to Berga.

You come down the hill from the town on the B-422, or turn onto it from the castle road. At the end of the straight there is a junction. You need to turn left (kind of back on yourself) on the C-1410z; it is not well signposted, but this is the Solsona direction. About a kilometre later, you will find the roundabouts that will put you onto the C-55 for Solsona and Andorra.

This is a straightforward, easy road which follows the river Cardener northward. It is not long before we get the first turning off that we can use, to get to 'NAVES'; there is one small sign low on your right just before the slip road, but the road doesn't have a number. It soon crosses the Cardener and then follows the Torrent de Sant Grau up into the hills through a long and pleasant, lightly wooded valley. It is quite narrow and bear in mind the possibility of timber lorries. The woods get thicker as we climb steadily, eventually coming out onto a higher plateau with big fields of cereals. Various little roads go off to small *pueblos* but stick with the 'main' road. Shortly after a 1.5 km long straight you will come to a 'T' junction with the slightly longer route to Navès via the dam for the Pantà de Sant Ponç and the *pueblo* of Linya.

The second route carries on up the C-55, past CLARIANA DE CARDENER (a very small *pueblo*) through a short tunnel until you get to the turning off to the right for 'Pantà de Sant Ponç *Direccio* Sta. Susanna'. Shortly arriving at a roundabout you take the first (right) exit for the Pantà. I do have to say that I hope you have not been spending too much time giggling in your helmet over place names; just remember, that pronounced in Spanish or Catalan they sound very different.

Once through the metropolis of under thirty houses, the road quickly enters a largely pine forest. It is probably timber lorries that have caused damage to the road surface which is a bit lumpy in places with the odd pothole so make sure you have time to take evasive action if required.

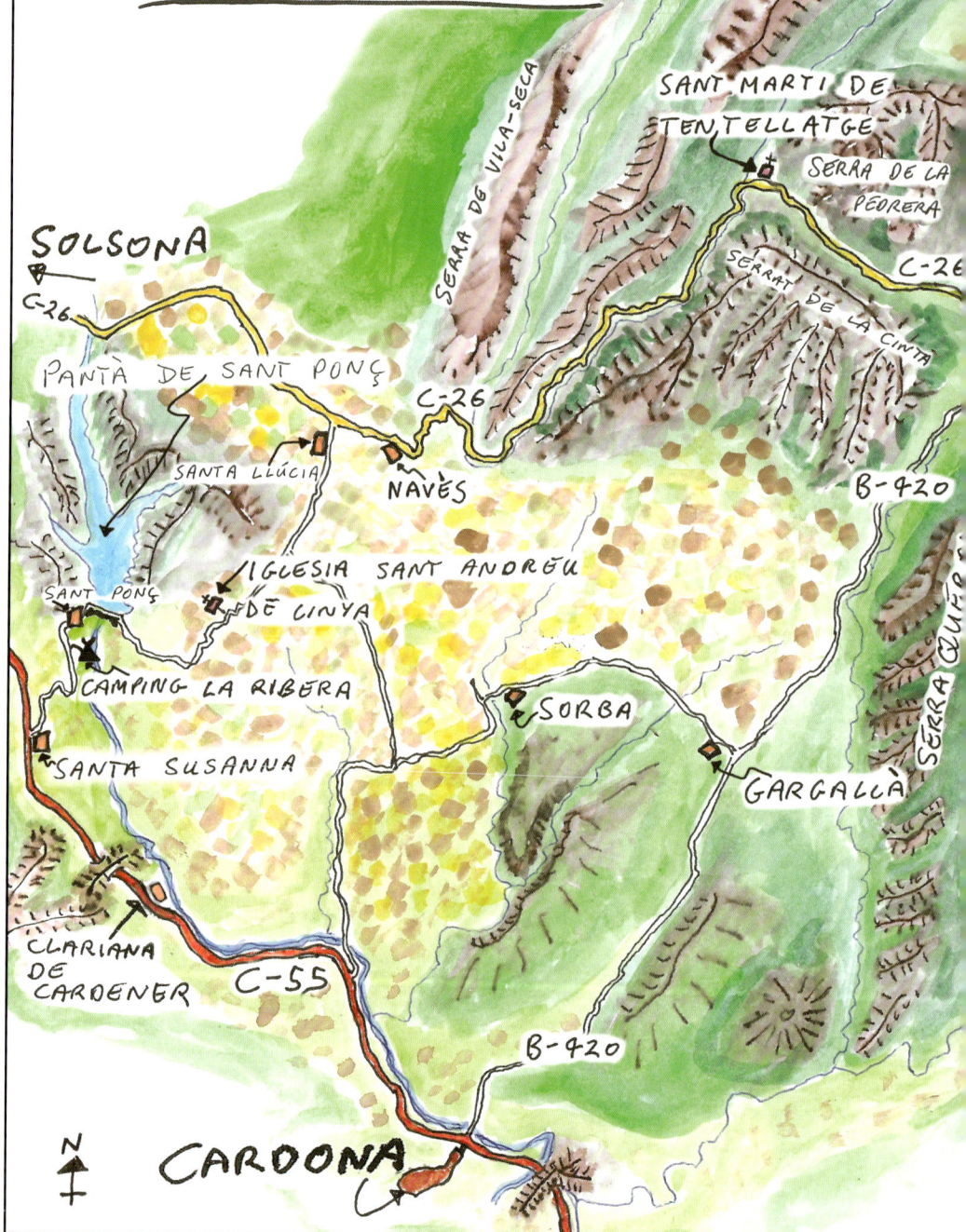

CARDONA TO
BERGA — 50 km

SANT MARTI DE
TENTELLATGE
SERRA DE LA
PEDRERA
SERRA DE VILA-SECA
C-26
SERRAT DE LA CINTA
SOLSONA
C-26
C-26
PANTÀ DE SANT PONÇ
B-420
SANTA LLÚCIA
NAVÈS
IGLESIA SANT ANDREU
DE LINYA
SANT PONÇ
SERRA QUEFRO
CAMPING LA RIBERA
SORBA
SANTA SUSANNA
GARGALLÀ
CLARIANA
DE
CARDENER
C-55
B-420
N
CARDONA

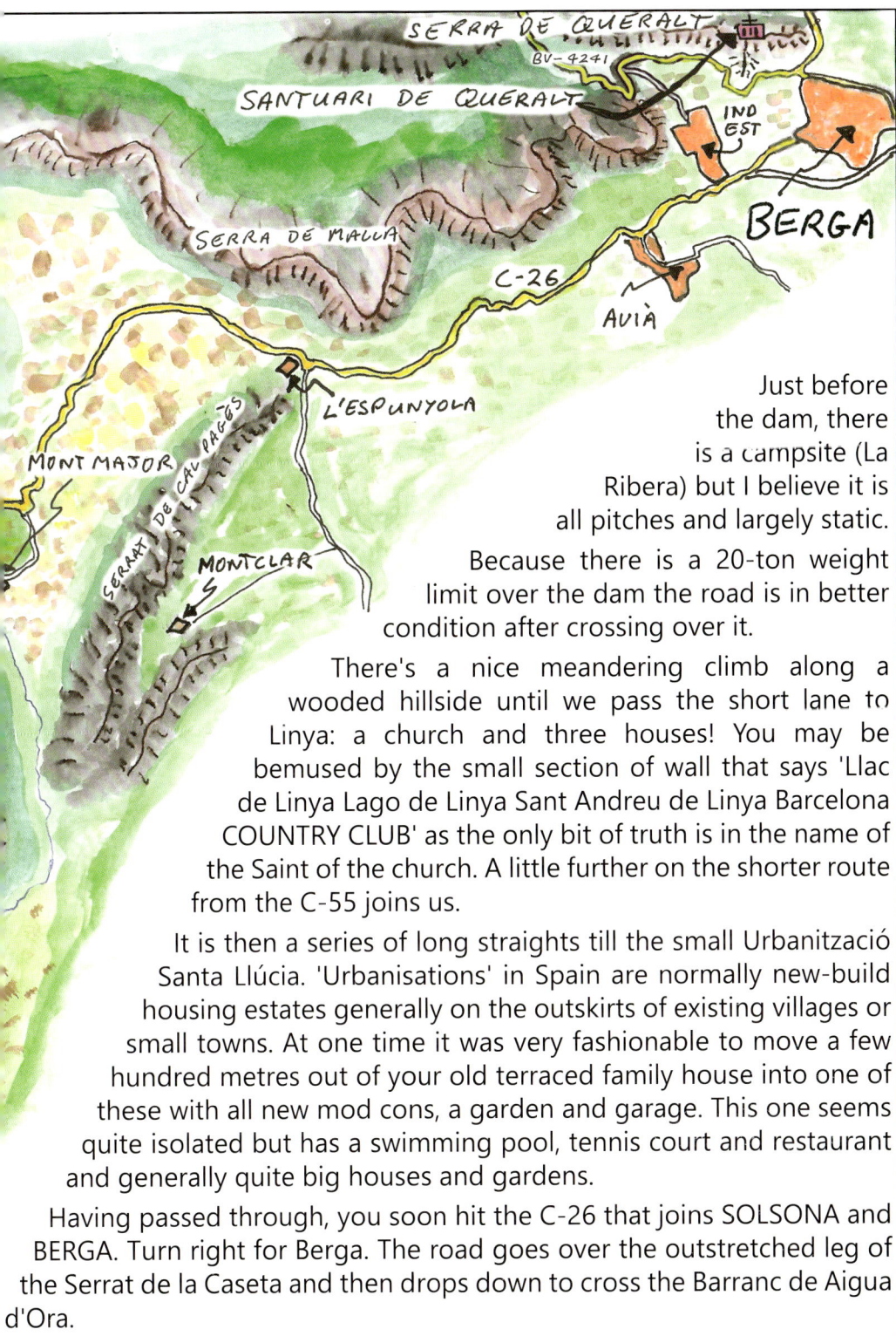

Map labels: SERRA DE QUERALT, BV-4241, SANTUARI DE QUERALT, IND EST, BERGA, SERRA DE MALLA, C-26, AVIÀ, L'ESPUNYOLA, MONT MAJOR, SERRAT DE CAL PAGÈS, MONTCLAR S

Just before the dam, there is a campsite (La Ribera) but I believe it is all pitches and largely static.

Because there is a 20-ton weight limit over the dam the road is in better condition after crossing over it.

There's a nice meandering climb along a wooded hillside until we pass the short lane to Linya: a church and three houses! You may be bemused by the small section of wall that says 'Llac de Linya Lago de Linya Sant Andreu de Linya Barcelona COUNTRY CLUB' as the only bit of truth is in the name of the Saint of the church. A little further on the shorter route from the C-55 joins us.

It is then a series of long straights till the small Urbanització Santa Llúcia. 'Urbanisations' in Spain are normally new-build housing estates generally on the outskirts of existing villages or small towns. At one time it was very fashionable to move a few hundred metres out of your old terraced family house into one of these with all new mod cons, a garden and garage. This one seems quite isolated but has a swimming pool, tennis court and restaurant and generally quite big houses and gardens.

Having passed through, you soon hit the C-26 that joins SOLSONA and BERGA. Turn right for Berga. The road goes over the outstretched leg of the Serrat de la Caseta and then drops down to cross the Barranc de Aigua d'Ora.

I do like trying to translate names like these and wonder about the stories behind them. The *serrat* is part of the verb *serrar* which is to 'saw' something. *Serra* or *sierra* (Catalan and Castillian) uses the teeth of the saw to make a mountain range. I think a *serrat* is a ridge. So, we go over the ridge of the little house or it could have been a toll booth, and down into the ravine of the water of Ora or of 'prayer' or even 'the hour'!

Anyway, next we follow the course of the Riera de Tentellatge another interesting one to figure out. *Tentellatge* in Catalan seems to mean 'foolishness' but has connotations of laughter and/or fluttering so I am going to go for the 'chuckling river'. Of course I could be completely wrong. It is a nice bit of road, curving its way along the hillside through a wooded valley.

The ridges to either side get higher and steeper and occasionally you can get glimpses of much higher mountains ahead. Then just before the green-roofed spire of the church of Sant Martí de Tentellatge, the C-26 turns east abandoning the Riera and skirting the feet of the Serra de la Pedrera and other *serrats* that come down from the Serra de Queralt which looms over Berga.

It takes half an hour or less to get to Berga, a pleasant open road of woods and fields that bring you past Avià to the entrance to the town. The steep comb-like cliffs of the top of the nearest *serrats* on your left contrast with the rolling plains that stretch away to the southward. At times it is possible to catch sight of the sharp teeth of Monserrat around 30 miles to the south.

Between the first and second roundabouts to your left is the LA VALLDAN Industrial Estate. The second roundabout has the C-26 going off to the right to bypass the town (signposted MANRESA and PUIGCERDA), while the C-149 continues straight on into the town itself.

It is quite a sprawling town with a population of around 16,000. The old town has the normal narrow streets, whilst you'll find wide boulevards and parks as you enter the new town. An Iberian tribe were centred here and Hannibal was their first recorded conqueror in 218 BC. They were obviously fairly independent types and rebelled twice against the Romans. Unfortunately, after their second defeat most of the tribe got sold into slavery.

In later times they came under the crown of Aragon.

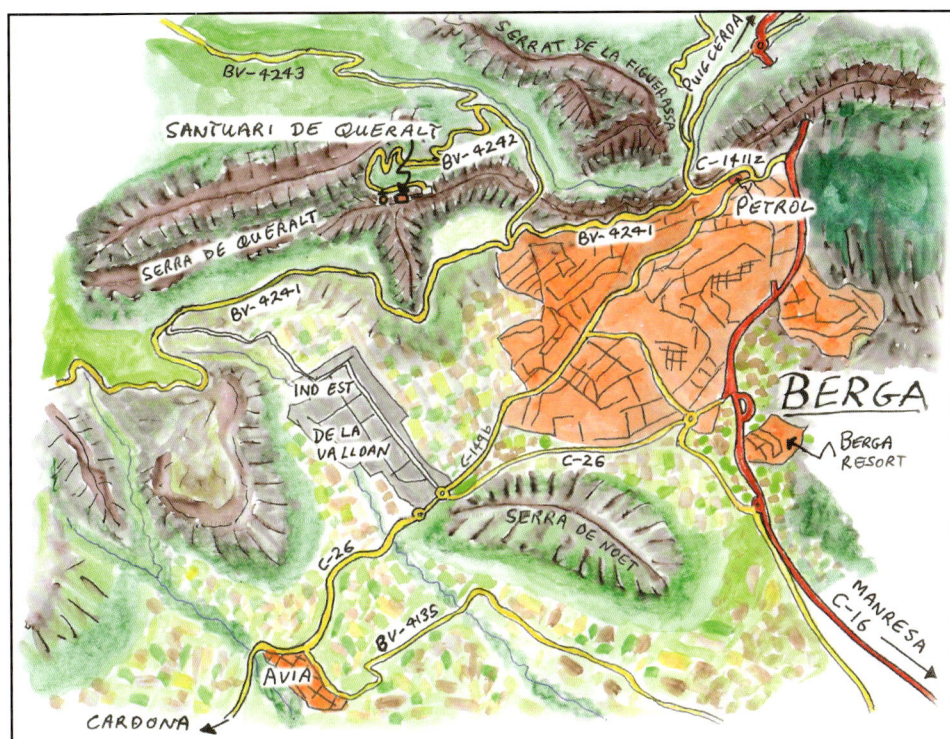

In 2012, proving some of the old spirit lived on, they declared King Juan Carlos 'persona non grata' after he went on an elephant hunt.

The Santuari de Queralt is perched high above the town on the first ridge of the Serra de Queralt. It has fantastic views and is well worth a visit.

One could go through the town and explore the old centre before getting out the other side and heading up, but the easiest way is to turn left (third exit) at the second roundabout into the LA VALLDAN Industrial Estate. Follow the road straight up through the estate to the top and turn left. Go to the end of the industrial units and the road bends round to the right, then turns into a single-track tarmac road heading for the mountain. This will snake you up to the BV-4241. At the STOP sign turn right; this great little road winds along the hillside above the town. Shortly you will come to a big sign that indicates left for the Santuari and Rasos de Peguera. Just round the corner is a kind of snaky crossroads where turning off left onto the BV-4242 will take you to the Santuari.

The BV-4241 goes straight on and with a few shenanigans with other road numbers, can drop you down into the town or connect you to the C-16 and C-26 which are the onward routes.

Right, drops you down into the top of Berga and if you used a satnav to guide you through the towns back streets, you could come up that way.

The road up to the Santuari is lovely, taking you round the end of the *serra* and then winding upward through cool forests till you arrive at the car park on top of the ridge. It is quite narrow and has sharp bends so do be aware that tourist coaches come up here and tend to take up most of the road or all of the corner!

Park up and you will immediately be drawn to the view. You are now just below three and a half thousand feet above sea level, with the town of Berga a thousand feet below you.

There is a little electric funicular cable car you can use to get up to the Santuari or just take your time climbing all the steps and enjoying the great view southward, where you should be able to pick out Monserrat easily.

The buildings are impressive and there is a bar but when I was there it only took cash. I was there in early July and was pleased with the occasional cooler breeze having gained that thousand feet. Beautiful Swallowtail and Brimstone butterflies distracted from the vast view. Do go the final stretch up the 190 steps to La Cova de la Mare de Déu de Queralt - The Cave of the Mother of God.

Berga from the Santuari de Queralt

The Route of the Cathars

This sanctuary is connected by trails with others that stretch all the way to Montségur in France. Montségur was the main stronghold of the Cathars, a pacifist Christian movement, that was the subject of the Albigensian Crusade called by Pope Innocent III to stamp out their so-called heresy. The 'heresy' included the belief that the spirit was genderless and that a spirit could be reborn as either man or woman, that both genders could, through their own devout beliefs, become *perfecti* 'pure in spirit' and thus be able to go to heaven permanently. This kind of equality was of course anathema to the Catholic Church and undermined their power and wealth directly. Added to this was the fact that the French King was quite happy to use the crusade against the Cathars (as well as the suppression by the Pope of the Knights Templar at around the same time) to take away the power and independence of various Counts and Lords of Languedoc allowing him to extend his control.

The Cathar trail follows the routes used by Cathar refugees in their attempt to escape persecutions. King Peter II of Aragon's sphere of influence included Languedoc and he allowed the Cathars to come and go. But then he joined in the fight against Simon de Montfort who, under the banner of the crusade, was attempting to carve himself his own Languedoc fiefdom. Unfortunately, Peter was killed at the battle of Muret (1213) when Raymond of Toulouse was defeated by Simon. The Cathars lost a lot of protection and their persecutions intensified leading to the destruction of Montségur (their strongest castle), the massacre of the inhabitants and the mass burning of over 200 *perfecti*.

I hope I haven't bored with my bit of history; for me, it always adds a bit of extra texture when you think of trying to attack huge castle walls or finding your way through those high mountains and forests to escape being burnt at the stake.

I am sure you could find many interesting shops and nice bars in Berga's old town and then take the easy straight route up the C-16 to the turning for Gósol and the spectacular mountain Pedraforca. But I have a detour in mind taking us through some great scenery further east to Ripoll.

So here is a decision point.

The fast (under an hour) route northward to Gósol is on the C-16 and is about 41 km (25 miles).

The Ripoll route is around 108 km (67 miles) and will take 2.5 hours, plus stops.

Either way, come back down the BV-4242 from the Santuari and turn left at the junction, onto the BV-4241 which crosses above the town and comes to a STOP junction. The turn left (onto the C-1411z) is signposted for MANRESA and BAGÀ as well as others including the Túnel del Cadí (more on that later).

You could also have come up here from the Centre Cíutat (town centre) which is down to the right. If you need petrol than turn right on the C-1411z (Centre Cíutat) and follow the bends down to a complex roundabout. 150 mts towards the town is the petrol station.

Berga to Gósol - 41 km (25 miles)

From the petrol station you can return to the roundabout and be directed onto the C-16 for PUIGCERDA and BARCELONA (see map on page 15).

Or take a more 'scenic' route northward using the C-1411z which is what the C-16 replaced. If you didn't need the petrol and turned left on the C-1411z after 800 mts you can use the BV-4654 (straight on) to join the C-16.

Or bear left sticking with the C-1411z for a more scenic route. It goes over and around instead of straight with tunnels. Good fun, but you do have to take a bit of care negotiating the small town of Cercs after which you are pushed back onto the C-16 anyway. This route runs alongside the Pantà de Baells at the top end of which, should you be there between October and November, you could enjoy the delights of the HORRORLAND theme park! Rather you than me... After that excitement there is about 5 miles of C-16 till the turn off to Saldes and Gósol just short of Guadiola de Berguedà.

See Map on page 20.

Berga to Gósol via Ripoll -108 km (67 miles)

So, having followed the BV-4654 to the interchange with the C-16, or come up from the petrol station, we are picking up the C-26. As long as the sun shines you won't regret it because it is a very interesting road that can be a major artery at times and at others, a very narrow vein. From here to Vilada it is just plain good fun. Running through forest across a long bridge over the Pantà de Baells, it follows the foot of the Pantà as it skirts the slopes of the Serra de Picancel. Vilada is a pleasant little town with a number of nice bars to stop at.

Continuing on eastward to Borreda, the road curves gently from side to side echoing the twists of the river El Mergançol about 50 mts to our right, which runs at the foot of the craggy *serra*. The woods are a mix of pine and deciduous, rich in wildlife; if you spot somewhere to stop, take a walk down to the river.

After a lovely 5 miles we turn away from the river to loop past Borreda: a tidy town of narrow streets and solid stone houses.

You will enjoy the next 26 km (15 miles) to Ripoll. Good tarmac, fields woods and meadows, the scent of pine, the scent of cut hay and a bend coming up. Maximise! Use the road you can see, to see the road you can't. READ the corner to its utmost and enjoy as well as being safe. We are staying in the valley bottom but that doesn't mean it is boring. Okay I had a perfect day weather wise, but those instincts that told me to take the long way round just because the map had some exceedingly wiggly bits on the GI-401 and then the B-402 from Ripoll back to Guardiola de Berguedà, were spot on.

Ripoll is quite a big spread out town. Situated at the junction of the rivers El Freser and Riu Ter. It has an interesting history from the Bronze Age onward. The Celts, Romans and Visigoths all developed the site. In the Early Middle Ages it grew in importance because there was coal, iron ore and plenty of water for metalworking. Apparently it supplied nails to the whole Iberian Peninsula. Then they moved on to armour and weaponry, then firearms. Unfortunately this made them a bit of a target and the French attacked in 1794, 1809, 1812 and 1813, all but destroying the industries. Finally, the Carlist civil wars from 1833 to 1876 caused almost total destruction. Luckily, the beautiful Romanesque Monastir de Santa Maria de Ripoll survived and is still at the heart of the largely rebuilt town. It has some wonderful cloisters and artefacts.

The C-16 and the C-17 run parallel to each other about 28 km (17 miles) apart, as the Griffon Vulture flies, but he doesn't follow the road. I also tried the Alpens route to Ripoll which was god fun. You can beat me to the Sant Jaume de Frontanyà cut through (but then you'd miss the REAL squiggles on the GI-402).

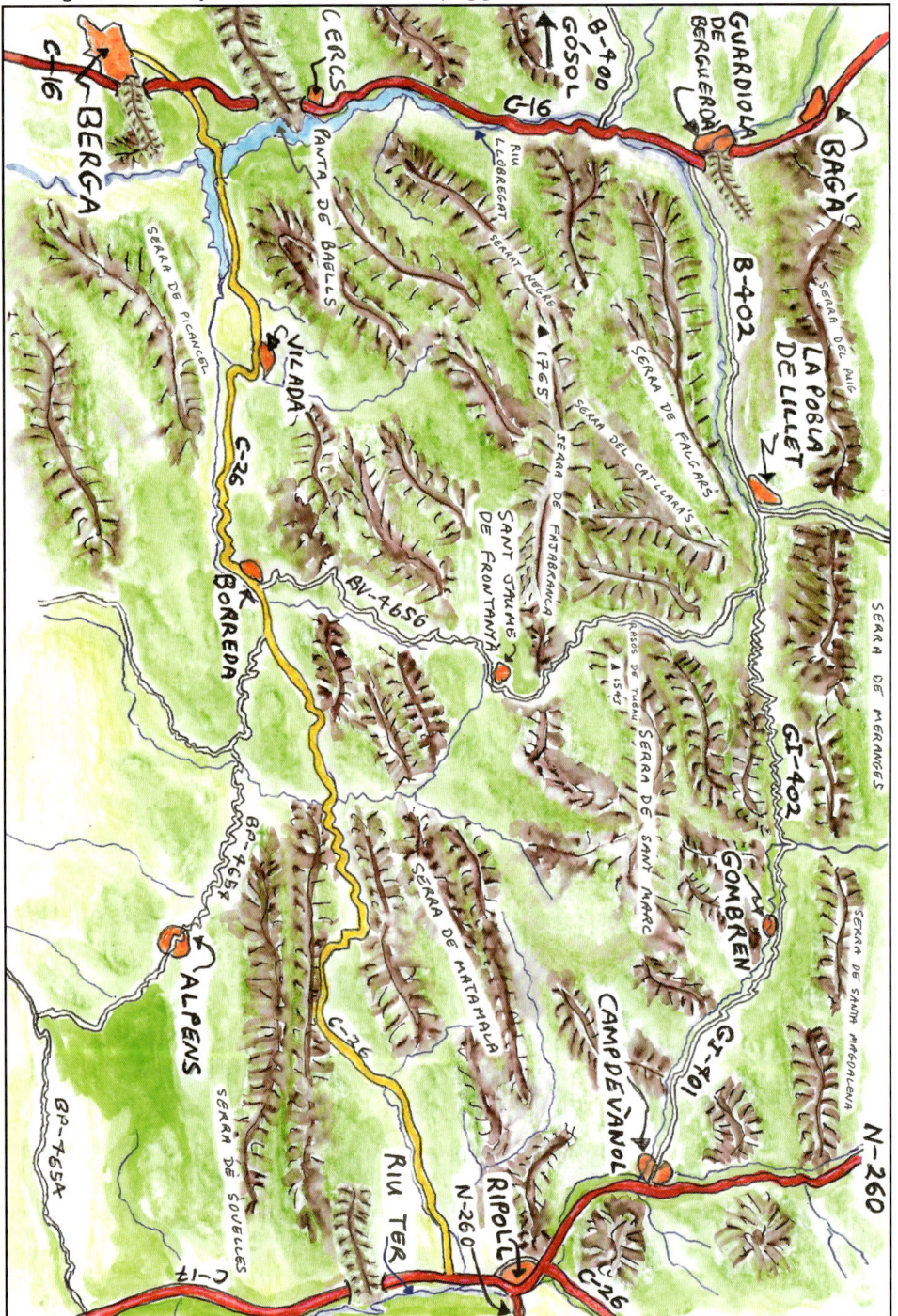

Approaching Ripoll, the C-26 has almost a mile-long dead straight at the end of which is a STOP junction with the C-17; turn left for RIPOLL. There is a petrol station half a mile up the road. At the second roundabout after it, you can choose to bypass the town by going left on the C-17 or go first right on the C-26 which, halfway through the right-hand side of the town, joins the N-260a and at the end of the town, joins with the C-17 and becomes the N-260 for CAMPDEVÀNOL and ANDORRA. Or, go straight ahead into the town.

I meandered my way through the town, which is quite a maze with many one-way streets. One of these brought me to a tiny *plaça* with a nice looking café under the birch trees. There was nowhere to park, so in true Spanish style I got on the pavement underneath the sign that said PROHIBIT APARCAR, and went to get my coffee. Within 5 minutes a Catalan couple on a bike joined me. I guess 6 bikes might have raised an eyebrow, but we had no problem.

There is another petrol station as you arrive at Campdevànol, which is where you need to turn off the N-260 onto what will be the GI-401. It is only at the junction that the number is signed. Before that, you need to look for the sign indicating Gombrèn and Centre Vila etc. to the left. This is just after a rocky bit of cliff close to the roadside on your right.

Follow the road straight through Campdevànol and out the other side. A long straight across the flood plain of the river El Merdàs ends at the foot of the Serra d l'Ós where we start following the contours of the valley bottom, the oaks and pines clothing the hillside above us. After 4 kilometres we start to climb onto the flanks of the *serra* and the views open out; rich farmland in the valley bottom a jumble of lush green hills that climb into the distance, glimpses of yet higher peaks beyond. In places, there is extensive terracing on the opposite side of the valley, though I couldn't work out what it was for.

The hillside here is very rocky with scrub and few trees, which means good visibility for the road ahead, and one can really enjoy all the corners I spotted on the map. By the time we get to Gombrèn we are around 900 mts (3,000') above sea level and the air is beautiful, warm but not too hot and scented with wild herbs and the tang of sun-baked rock.

Gombrèn is a small village really, with most of it down to the left below: bend right around the church and one is leaving. As the road climbs away along the mountainside you will see a blue sign that says Coll de Merolla; hopefully below it a green sign 'OBERT', just a little reminder that in winter many of these roads can be closed by snow and ice. The Coll itself is another 6 km of great road away and another 600 feet higher on what is now the GI-402.

The Refugi Coll de Merolla at the top has a restaurant and is recommended by local bikers. A little further on is the Casa Rural Mas Merolla. If there was a group of you that wanted to have a weekend in one place then this might be a good possibility; up to 6 people from Friday to Sunday costs around €550 (2019). It is well appointed and has fantastic views; you can see the toothy peaks of Pedraforca in the distance.

A 'Casa Rural' in Iberia can be a rural B&B or a whole house that you can rent (generally for a minimum of two nights), often beautifully done up and in a rural setting. They can take a little bit of research and advance booking but can be a very pleasant and more independent alternative to hostels, hostals (small family-run hotels) or hotels.

More lovely snaky mountainside road, a number change to B-402 and eventually we drop down into La Pobla de Lillet: a place to remember as we are coming back here to take the long mountain detour around the expensive Tunnel de Cadi, which is on the C-16 route to Vielha.

And as you come to the little town you will see the turning to the right (BV-4031) with various signs. HELIPORT is the first then CASTELLAR DE N'HUG and LA MOLINA as well as the source (Les Fonts) of the main river El Llobregat, which is the tunnel avoidance route. Just past this junction there is a handy petrol station should you need it.

Pedraforca seen in the distance from the B-402

The stretch of mountains down to Guardiola de Berguedà are formed of marls and sandstones but also gypsum, all great stuff for cement, and the quarries and their associated industry are very obvious in the landscape around Pobla. If you continue through the little town (population around a 1,000) on the main road, about 1 km beyond there is a the narrow gauge railway museum and station - Ferrocarril Turístic de l'Alt Llobregat. It can be well worth taking the time to stop because this little Tren del Ciment is great fun.

It runs from the beginning of April to the end of November (check timetables at www.trendelciment.cat/en/timetables-prices/) and a combined ticket of €13.40 (adult) includes the Jardins Artigas and Museu del Ciment. Now you might not be getting all excited about the prospect, but bear with me.

To start with, the train runs on a kind of tramway in the road right through the town. Pedestrians and cars having to get out of the way! You can hop off in the town which has some interesting Romanesque and medieval architecture as well as plenty of bars and restaurants. Continuing on the train, in less than a mile you get to the Jardins Artigas, a park designed by Antoni Gaudí and built between 1905 and 1906. I am always fascinated by Gaudí's use of the natural form and reinforced concrete. The Sagrada Familia in Barcelona is of course his major work but there many other intriguing examples of his extraordinary ideas. The Count of Güell was a big sponsor of Gaudí and engaged him to design a housing unit for technicians of the Catllaràs coal mines (a few miles south of La Pobla) which supplied the cement factory.

The Artigas family lent Gaudí their house whilst he was doing the work and in return he designed the gardens for them. Take a pleasant wander round taking in the arches and Catholic symbols typical of his work.

Next on the train journey is the Museu del Ciment Asland de Castellar de n'Hug, also known as the Clot del Moro Museum. It was in operation from 1904 until 1975. It is an extraordinary collection of buildings that cling to the mountainside between the railway and the quarry above, using gravity to facilitate the cement production. Considering the pretty extreme winters this high in the Pyrenees, it was a major endeavour but one that was very important for the industrial growth of Catalonia in the 20th century. You can visit the cement museum by road instead of using the train.

I have a note in my journal from somewhere on this road and I think it was in La Pobla : "Lady Godiva on an 'L' plate in a negligee!" I have this memory of a scooter going in the opposite direction with a very 'scantily' clad lady looking very composed and with a big smile on her face. These moments are the absolute spice of being a traveller.

I also noted having to take evasive action from a group of identical green Kawasaki sports bikes all following the leaders line/back tyre; his line was fine as he cut the corner before I got there, the followers were in my road space. Don't blindly follow the vehicle ahead!

It is a pleasant 10-minute run down the B-402 to Guardiola de Berguedà. At the first roundabout, go left (third exit) for GUARDIOLA. Shortly there is another roundabout over the top of the C-16 which we can now take southward for BERGA and BARCELONA.

A couple of kilometres (a little over a mile) and you will see a footbridge over the road and then signs for the turning we want, to the right. First, Massis del Pedraforca and then VALLCEBRE, SALDES and GÓSOL on the B-400. Pedraforca is one of the main reasons for this detour as it is a spectacular mountain.

As soon as you get round the first corner you know this is going to be good fun. We cross a bridge over a river (the rocky Ríu de Saldes) and start winding our way through wooded hillsides. If it is really hot, do watch out for the 'tar snakes' in the road as they can melt and become rather slippery. After 4 km we come to the Torrent de Bosoms (more fun with place names), see the map for the little places you can stop to enjoy it (them).

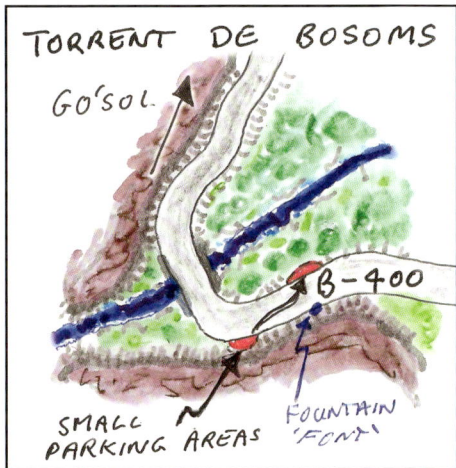

TORRENT DE BOSOMS
GÓSOL
B-400
SMALL PARKING AREAS
FOUNTAIN 'FONT'

GO'SOL AND PEDRAFORCA

We are climbing up the side of a small hill, with the Ríu de Saldes below on our right. Above it the Serra de Gisclareny which goes up to 1538 mts (5,000'). Beyond that is the massive wall of the Serra de Cadí-Moixeró range which is about 50 km (30 miles) long and goes up over 2,500 mts (8,000'). It cuts us off from the valley of the Segre river which runs between La Seu d'Urgell and Puigcerdà. The C-16 from Bagà goes underneath through the misnamed Tunel de Cadí (it actually goes under the Serra de Moixeró) and is the most expensive tunnel in Iberia! It costs nearly €10 for a motorbike and just over €12 for a car. Hence my detour route from La Pobla to La Molina. Of course that will cost you more than the tunnel in petrol but it is much more fun and anyway, it is the principle...

We are getting into the Parc Natural del Cadí-Moixeró and as we wind through the forest it won't be long before you catch glimpses of Pedraforca. I think that you could translate this from the Catalan as the 'stone pitchfork'. Coming from this direction, you get the full effect of its isolation and the two sharp, naked rock summits, both of which are over 8,000' (2,450 and 2,416 mts).

There are lots of places to stay around here, with a number of campsites, hostals and hotels. It is a very popular area for hiking and

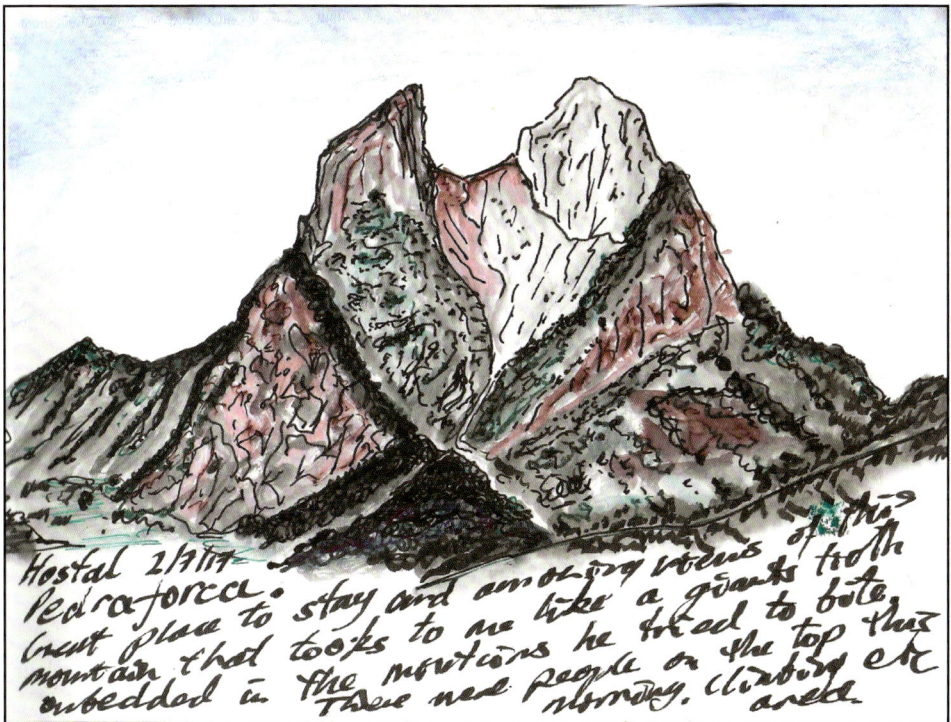

Hostal 2/7/17 Pedraforca. great place to stay and amazing views of this mountain that looks to me like a giants tooth embedded in the mountains he tried to bite. There are people on the top this morning. Climbing etc area.

so it might be worth booking in advance in the season. I have stayed at the Hostal Pedraforca which was very nice, but does get booked up on the weekends.

You will see the sign for it (off left) just after you have passed the little *pueblo* of Maçaners.

Before you get to the next *pueblo* Saldes, you will find a Repsol petrol station with a small shop and café. Six miles beyond Saldes on the other side of the mountain you will come to Gósol. By the roundabout at the entrance to the *pueblo* you will find the Hostal Cal Fransisco, a friendly family-run hotel with 24 rooms. Having stayed for a night in 2018 I was remembered and welcomed in 2019. I happened to arrive on the eve of San Juan (St John) which is a fiesta night with bonfire and fireworks; his birthday on the 24th is a public holiday in Catalonia.

First thing to do was have a cold beer on the terrace at the back of the hotel with its great views. I soon realised it was going to be a noisy night as fireworks were already being set off, the blasts echoing off the mountainsides. A little later, I walked into the village and got talking to Flora and her son at the Bar de la Plaça on one side of the small square.

As it got dark a bonfire was lit in the square and the frequency of bangs and rockets increased. I was sure there was going to be an accident as all the kids seemed to have a carrier bag of assorted fireworks, and little gas lighters to set them off with. Watching a four-year-old squatting over a firework made my blood run cold. However, there were not any incidents as far as I know. There was going to be a traditional communal pie (*cena publica*) to eat later on, but having had a long hot day of travel I decided to quit about half eleven. The next day when I had a coffee and sketched at the bar, the son told me the fiesta had wound down at three in the morning but he had then gone on to another one that finished at six in the morning. I'm getting old...

Pedraforca from the Bar de la Plaça in Gósol

Excursions from Gósol

If you are able to spend a couple of days here there is a lot to explore. Take a hike up Pedraforca for instance.

Or visit Josa de Cadí a small *pueblo* about ten minutes further west from Gósol on the road to Tuixent, (which is in Book 2 of this series). It is well worth a visit for its pretty cobbled streets and the views from the interesting church, built on the highest point of the rock on which the village perches. It feels steeped in history and is again on the Cathar escape routes.

Josa de Cadí

If you would like a bit of an adventure then you could continue on to Tuixent, head north a short way on the C-462 towards Cornellana and La Seu d'Urgell but turn off after about 3 km onto what becomes the LV-4001 for "Moli de F. SORRIBES DE LA VANSA and Ossera". From this junction it is 33 km (20-odd miles) to Pont de la Torre on the El Segre river that comes down from La Seu d'Urgell. Amazing views but the middle section is (or was in 2018) a gravel track. See photos opposite.

You could make a circuit by heading up the C-14 to La Seu d'Urgell and come back to Tuixent on the C-462. This is detailed in Book 2 and is part of the *Moturisme* route 5.

You can see the switchback you will be taking on the near right-hand hillside

Hard gravel roadway for the middle section, nothing extreme

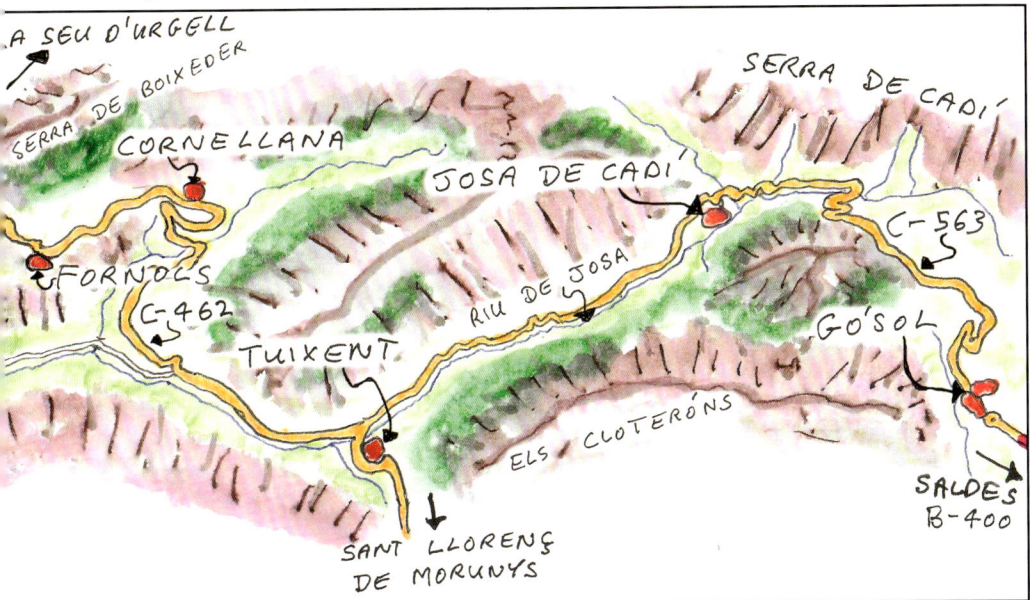

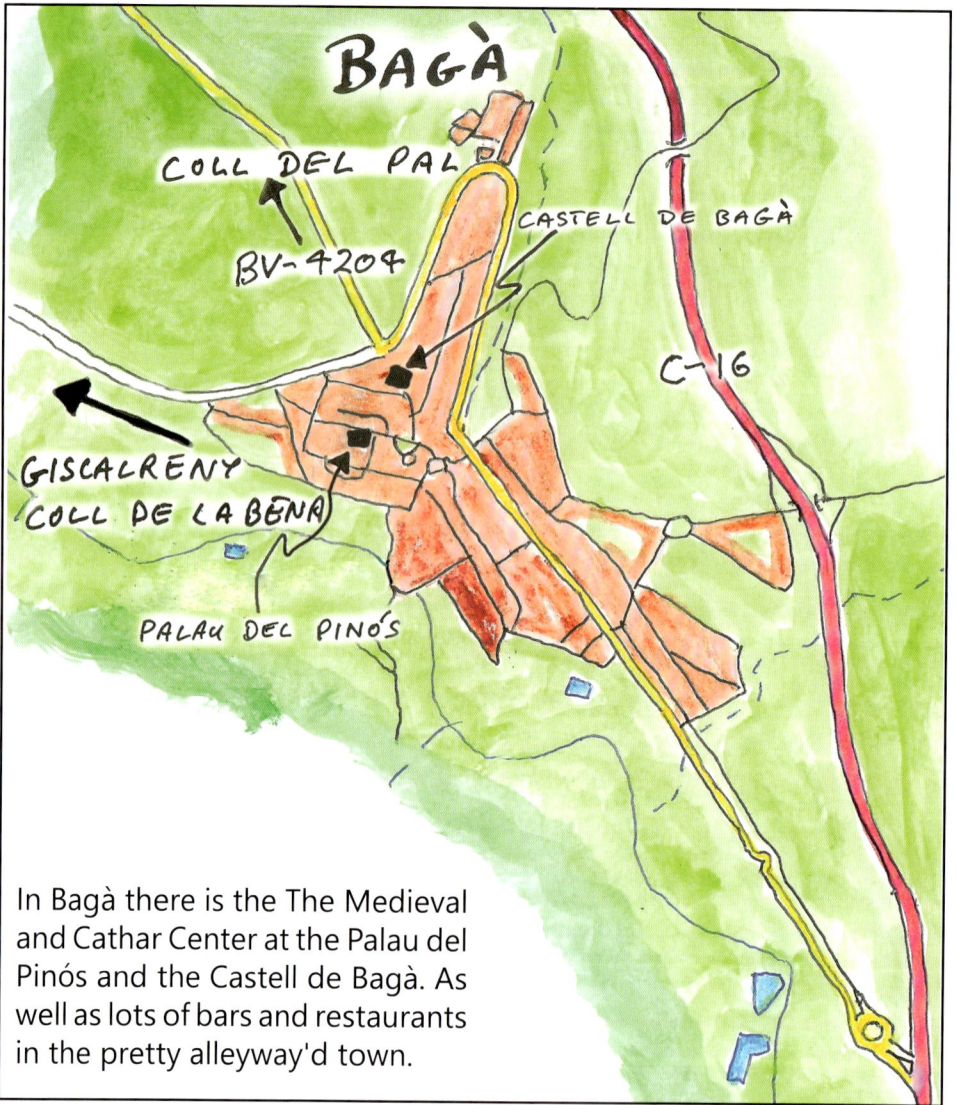

BAGÀ

COLL DEL PAL

BV-4204

CASTELL DE BAGÀ

C-16

GISCALRENY
(COLL DE LA BENA)

PALAU DEL PINÓS

In Bagà there is the The Medieval and Cathar Center at the Palau del Pinós and the Castell de Bagà. As well as lots of bars and restaurants in the pretty alleyway'd town.

If visiting Bagà you could also try out a circular route with some more dirt roads. Though I have not completed this route it should be possible. You could do it either way round: starting at Saldes or at Bagà. See maps opposite. If starting from Bagà, go to the top of the town and take the unnumbered road signposted for Gisclareny (Av Reina Elisenda and then Av. del Districe Forestal). This passes the Camping Bastalreny on the way up to Coll de la Bena where the tarmac ends, at 1430 mts (4,700'). Two reasonable looking dirt tracks continue onward, the left-hand one goes west and I think you should be able get through to the Mirador de Gresolet where tarmac starts again, and

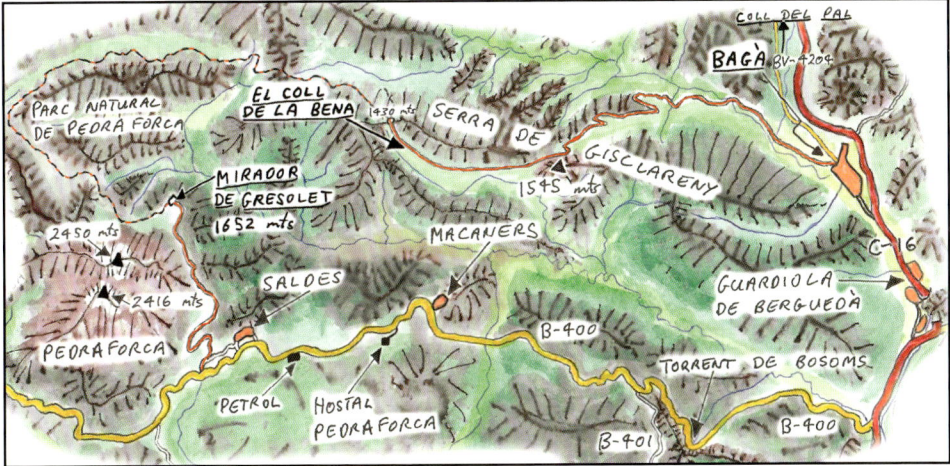

come down onto the B-400 near Saldes. El Coll de la Bena has a Casa Rural and a restaurant but I doubt they are open all year round.

You could also take a trip up to the Coll del Pal which is 2108 mts (nearly 7,000') high at the end of the BV-4024. This is a spectacular road with fantastic views and hairpin bends with sheer drops from craggy cliffs.

A bit past the actual Coll the tarmac ends and dirt roads continue; who knows where...

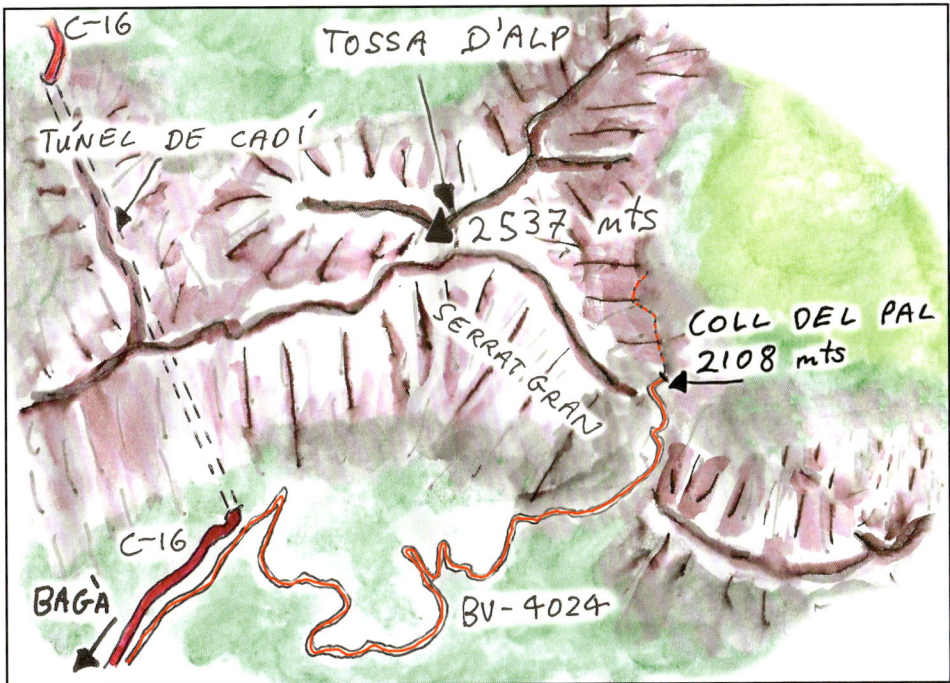

Gósol to La Seu d'Urgell - 120 km (74 miles)

If you were short of time, you could go to La Seu d'Urgell via Tuixent which would take about an hour and a bit (53 km - 33 miles).

The long way round will take 2.5 hrs without stops. The first thing is to retrace the route to La Pobla de Lillet. At Guardiola de Berguedà you could pop up to Bagà and the Cathar museum or, take the C-16 on through the Tunel de Cadí which cuts off 40 km and saves the time and fuel of the La Pobla route over the top of the Serra de Montgrony.

At La Pobla de Lillet you have a second opportunity to visit any of the points of interest there. At the far side of La Pobla, we are going to turn left up the BV-4301 for Castellar de n'Hug. The road clings to the steep hillside above the Lobregat river and within a couple of miles you will see the Cement Museum on your left; there is a turning for it and you could take the train from here down to Jardins Artigas and La Pobla.

Castellar de n'Hug is about 15 minutes beyond the museum, climbing all the way and passing first through the narrow gap of the Pas de l'Ós. By the way, that 'Ós' is a bear! And there are some large Brown Bears around up here; if you are very lucky you might see one.

This is a great section of road through forest with the river down to your right and occasional glimpses of big peaks ahead. Within a kilometre you pass a cutting in the rock at the point where one kind of rock strata changes to another; a grey gypsum to a chocolate brown red silt or claystone (I am guessing at the rock types). Around the next corner the road crosses a wide flat area where the flesh and bones of the mountain are exposed, by the erosion of the thin layer of struggling vegetation. It feels like it could almost be the site of a landslip. One of those times when I wish I knew more about geology.

After crossing this area the road climbs onto the flank of the mountain above the river El Lobregat and a mile or so later we come to the Hostal les Fonts. 'Les Fonts' is Catalan for 'the sources' and there is a pretty old arched bridge where El Lobregat, now a small stream tumbles down the mountainside next to the hotel. The hostal has great food and facilities but not that many rooms, so if you are thinking of staying then pre-book.

About 3 km further and rounding a corner, Castellar comes into view. It's a typical jumble of houses and roofs that are terraced up a hillside. It is great to wander through the historic centre, and there are many

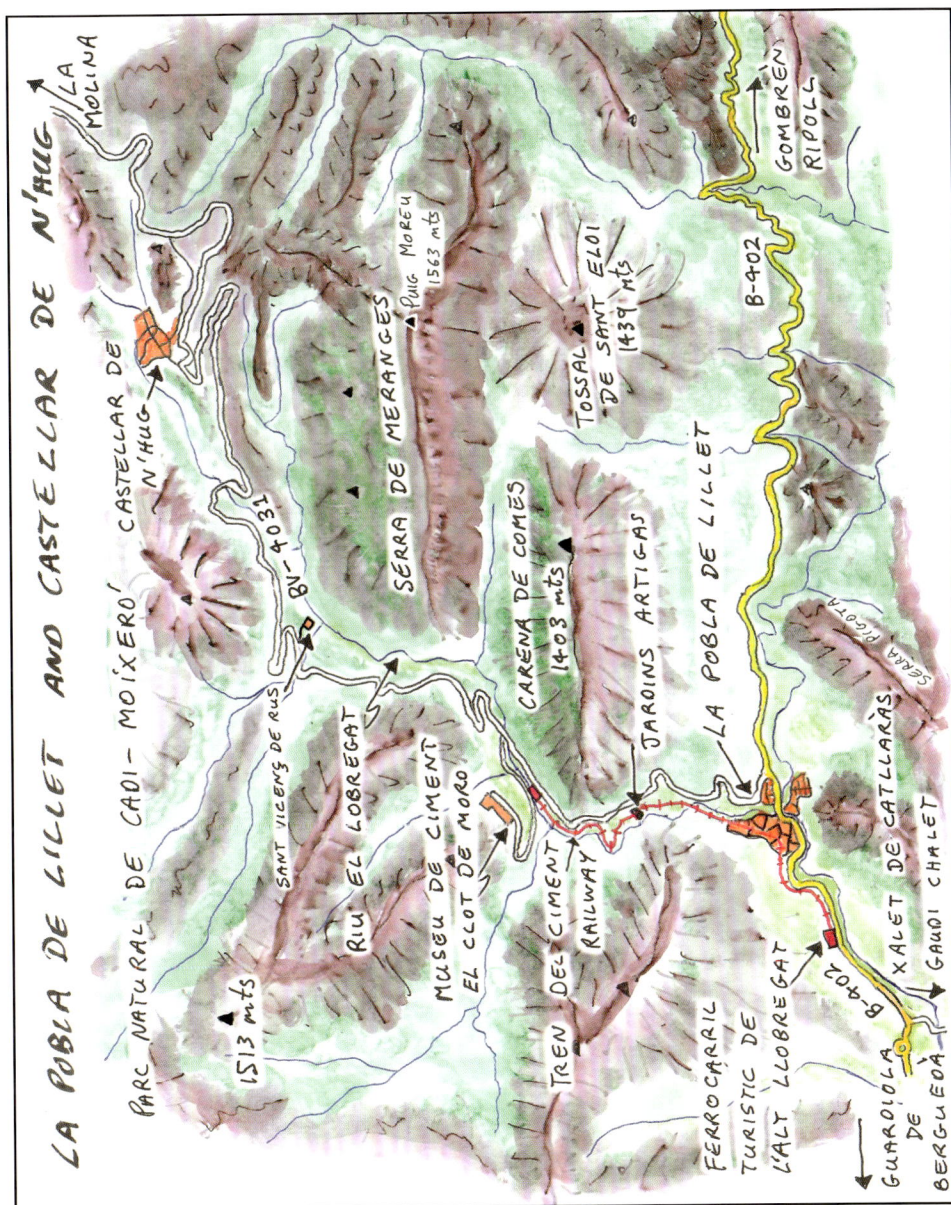

LA POBLA DE LILLET AND CASTELLAR DE N'HUG

PARC NATURAL DE CADI- MOIXERO/ CASTELLAR DE N'HUG

LA MOLINA

GOMBREN / RIPOLL

B-402

PUIG MOREU 1563 mts

SERRA DE MERANGES

TOSSAL DE SANT ELOI 1439 mts

SERRA PICOSA

CARENA DE COMES 1403 mts

JARDINS ARTIGAS

LA POBLA DE LILLET

BV-4031

SANT VICENS DE RUS

RIU EL LLOBREGAT

MUSEU DE CIMENT / EL CLOT DE MORO

TREN DEL CIMENT / RAILWAY

1513 mts

XALET DE CATLLARAS

GAUDI CHALET

FERROCARRIL TURISTIC DE L'ALT LLOBREGAT

B-402

GUARDIOLA DE BERGUEDA

bars, restaurants and shops selling all sorts of local produce. The town hosts a number of fiestas and events that just might be happening when you arrive. If you want to go into the town, you need to take a left at the point where the main road for La Molina (indicated straight on) bends quite sharply round to the right.

There are some great views as the road follows a ridge at around 5,000' and these are the 'foothills' of the main range of the Serra de la Moíxera, the top of which La Creueta, is 2067 mts (6,872').

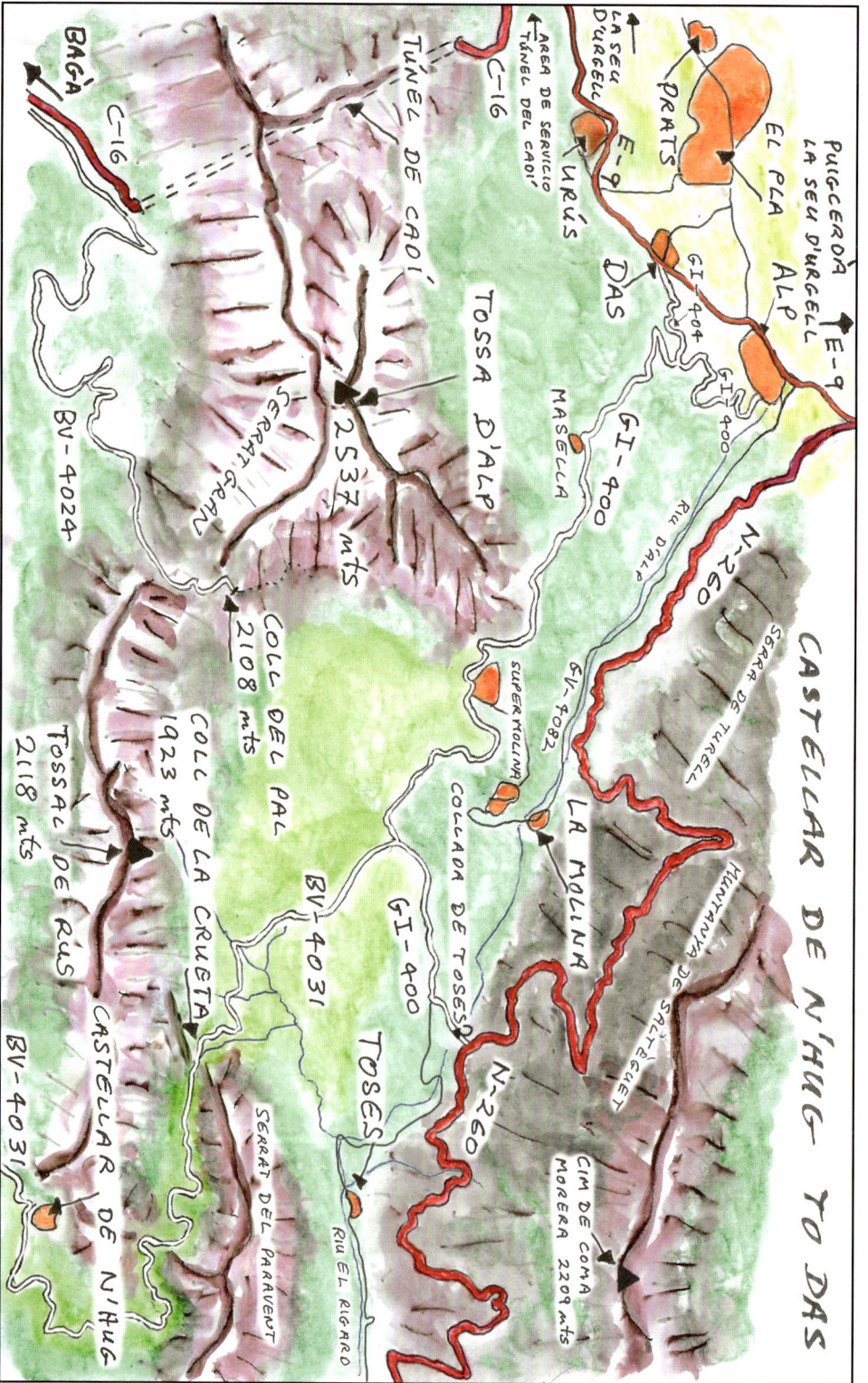

CASTELLAR DE N'HUG TO DAS

PUIGCERDÀ
LA SEU D'URGELL
LA SEU D'URGELL
PRATS
EL PLA
ALP
E-9
E-9
BAGÀ
C-16
C-16
C-16
ÀREA DE SERVICIO TÚNEL DEL CADÍ
TÚNEL DE CADÍ
URÚS
DAS
ALP
GI-404
GI-400
BV-4024
SERRAT GRAN
TOSSA D'ALP
2537 mts
MASELLA
GI-400
RIU D'ALP
N-260
COLL DEL PAL 2108 mts
COLL DE LA CRUETA 1923 mts
SUPER MOLLINA
BV-4082
LA MOLINA
SERRA DE TARRELLA
COLLADA DE TOSES
BV-4031
GI-400
MUNTANYA DE SALTEGUET
TOSSAL DE RUS 2118 mts
CASTELLAR DE N'HUG
BV-4031
SERRAT DEL PARAVENT
TOSES
RIU EL RIGARD
N-260
CIM DE COMA MORERA 2209 mts

Reaching the flanks of the *serra* the road climbs steadily to the west, the mountainside reminiscent of the short grass and occasional gorse bushes of the Brecon Beacons. As long as we are not in a cloud, there are huge vistas of mountain ranges southward that we are now on a level with or above. Also places where you can spot the teeth of Pedraforca in the distance.

The highest point of the road is at the Coll de Creueta 1923 mts (6,300') from where mountain ranges roll to the horizon in all directions. A high and wide country, sweeping bends, great tarmac and amazing vistas of the piled high Pyrenees.

The road now takes its time dropping down towards the valley; these long gentle slopes of short grass must make for fantastic skiing in the winter, the snow poles beside the road indicate the liability of deep and drifted snow. Just before we drop down into the wooded valley, there is the Collada del Pedró ski station.

Looking north just after Coll de Creueta

Past the ski station, the BV-4031 meets the GI-400 giving a choice of two routes between here and Bellver de Cerdanya.

The longer but easier route means turning right on the GI-400 for RIPOLL and GIRONA, crossing the Collada de Toses to the N-260 and turning left for PUIGCERDÀ. It is a great road that wiggles for 10 miles along the flanks of the mountainside at the top of which runs the French border. At Puigcerdà stick with the N-260 going west for La Seu d'Urgell and Andorra.

The shorter but more fiddly route goes left on the GI-400 past La Molina and Masella, twiddling nicely along the mountainside before dropping down towards Alp. There is a junction here with the GI-404 which you turn left onto for DAS (8t weight limit). Very shortly there is a STOP junction with the E-9 (Das itself is on the other side) here you turn left signed BARCELONA (via the expensive tunnel).

Now it does get fiddly as you can see from the map below: you are forced onto the C-16 southbound (Tunnel) and have to go a long way round the service area to head back northward for LA SEU D'URGELL, ANDORRA and PUIGCERDÀ. At the service slip road it does have a sign for RIU DE CERDANYA and a little later LA SEU etc. Having managed not to get stuffed into the tunnel, the C-16 will shortly join up with the N-260 just before Bellver de Cerdanya. And it is now a straightforward and enjoyable 34 km (20 miles) run to La Seu d'Urgell.

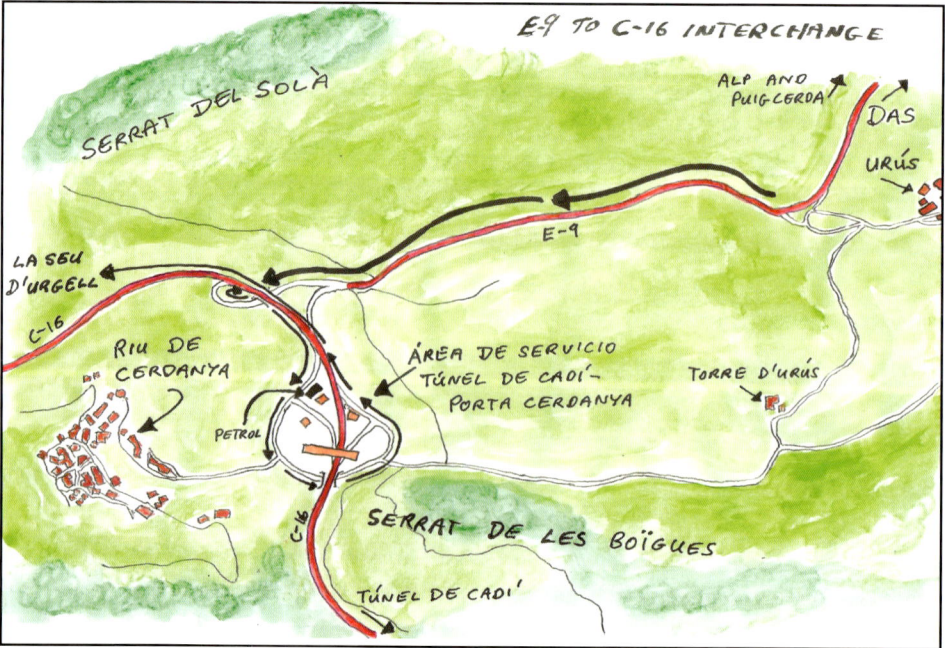

E-9 TO C-16 INTERCHANGE

SERRAT DEL SOLÀ

ALP AND PUIGCERDA

DAS

URÚS

E-9

LA SEU D'URGELL

C-16

RIU DE CERDANYA

ÀREA DE SERVICIO
TÚNEL DE CADÍ-
PORTA CERDANYA

TORRE D'URÚS

PETROL

C-16

SERRAT DE LES BOÏGUES

TÚNEL DE CADÍ

La Seu d'Urgell

La Seu is on the main route to Andorra and is also detailed in other books in this series.

As befits an important centre for a large surrounding area, La Seu has many markets and fiestas. Weekly markets are held every Tuesday and Saturday in the Main Street and various fiestas through the year. In October there is the Fira de Sant Ermengol, which is said to be the oldest in Spain and includes the Fira de Formatges Artesans del Pirineu (A Pyrenean cheese festival and market). In July there is the Mercat Medieval dels Canonges, a festival of street music, theatre, circus and falconry, and twice a year in March and September the Mercat de les Opportunitats. So when you have an idea of your itinerary, it might be worth checking online to see if it coincides with an event. The *centro historico* is well worth exploring; the cathedral cloisters are lovely and the bell tower impressive. The Plaça del Deganat is a nice space to amble in, people watch and not be travelling.

On the edge of the town is a 300-metre white water competition course, using the El Segre river, which was built for the 1992 Barcelona Olympics. The course uses turbines that can push the flow rate up by 12 m^3/s but cleverly, when not being used in this way, they are reversed and used to generate electricity for the town.

To the west of the town and dominating it, is Castellciutat, worth exploring, if you have the time. The roads are narrow and a bit confusing but getting up to the car park at the top of the settlement is fairly obvious. The views of the remains of the 9th-century fortress with the mighty backdrop of the Pyrenees beyond are impressive. The hill of Castellciutat was the original settlement then called Arse-durgui (no comment). The spur of rock conveniently dominating the confluence of the Segre and Gran Valira rivers was called Puiolo Urgelli, and this gave its name when the city of Urgell was built (in Latin, Civitas Orgellia and in Catalan, Ciutat d'Urgell). The Hotel Castell de Ciutat is next to the fortress ruins and is top quality. But in 2018 I stayed in the Hotel Nice in the city centre. The hotel underground car park is down the side street opposite; unfortunately it is a 'One-Way', the wrong way. I have to admit to doing a 'naughty' and going the wrong way rather than finding my way around. On a motorbike nobody seemed bothered. By the way, be aware that there is a lower door at the bottom of the ramp. If it is shut it could be a problem for you as there is no level area by the door to stop the bike whilst getting the door opened. There are plenty of other hotels in the town and a campsite on the N-260 west, just after the Industrial Estate.

Castelcuitat

La Seu d'Urgell to Sort - 50 km (30 miles)

This is easy as it is all on the N-260 and will take an hour or so without stops. Leaving La Seu, we head south-west on the N-260 for ADRALL and LLEIDA. Passing under the Castellciutat there is a long 5 km (3 mile) straight to Adrall where the C-14 continues south for Lleida and Barcelona, but we will take the first exit at the roundabout staying with the N-260 for SORT and EL PONT DE SUERT.

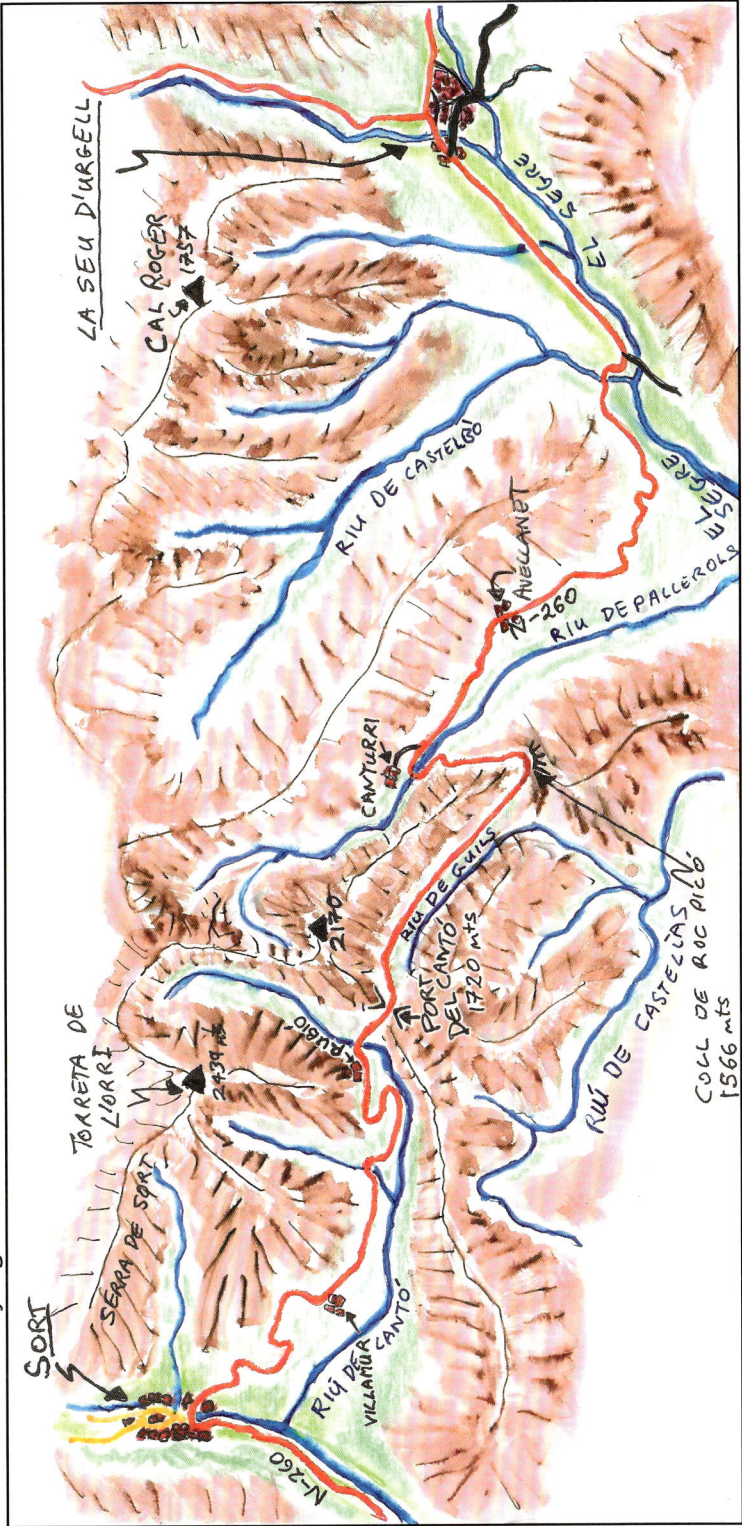

Col de Roc Picó

By the way, I have seen Guardia Civil or Policia Local doing checks here more than once, possibly of traffic from Andorra or France but also, perhaps, speed checks on that long straight.

A couple of fields and then the road starts up a loosely wooded mountainside turning up the valley of the Riu de Pallerols. There are a few nice hairpin bends and if you stop, some great views back down into the valley of El Segre.

As we round the shoulder of the Serrat de la Curna at 1125 mts (3,700'), the road becomes faster with easier bends, rising through low woodland that allows glimpses of wide vistas. We arrive at Avellanet and the road squeezes through its stone walls, and then contours

Port El Cantó

around the head of the Riu de Pallerols with steep rocky hillsides above and below.

After a couple of hairpin bends and a long reach across the forested mountainside, we come to the Col de Roc Picó at 1546 mts (5,000'). There is a lay-by and Mirador on the outside of the bend but coming from this direction you cannot enter it. If you want to stop here just 200 metres round the corner there is a side road to Guils de Cantó where you can turn round and come back to the lay-by. The views are superb as you look out across the expanse of the Pallerols valley to the road we came up on; you can even pick out the *pueblos* of Avellanet and Pallerols del Cantó. Of course when exiting you will have to go

about 500 metres in the wrong direction before there is a little dirt parking spot you can turn around on.

The next 7 km or so are pretty straight and even running along the Serrat de Carlà above the valley of the Riu de Guils. Eventually we reach the col at the head of the Riu de Guils, the Port El Cantó at 1720 mts (5,643'). There is plenty of lay-by to pull into and if you feel like a little adventure, take one of the dirt roads that go off to either side into the open and scrubby mountain hillsides.

Continuing, we drop 500' to the tiny *pueblo* (20 houses) of Rubió. You catch glimpses of house roofs above the road where it bends round a big red cliff that is obviously somewhat unstable as it is massively netted. Just around the corner and after the turning to the *pueblo* is the Restaurant Rubió: yet another great place to stop for a coffee or some excellent food.

Three slight bends later and there is a long straight at the end of which is the parking for the Despoblat Medieval de Santa Creu de Llagunes. The excavated ruins of a medieval village built on a Bronze Age site. It has amazing views and is not expensive to visit (€2 single, €5 guided and €7 if you catch the 'Theatrical Tour' on a Friday at 11.30). There is a small museum in the next little *pueblo* of Llagunes.

View from Port Ainé

The N-260 here skirts the Toretta de L'Orri peak which at 2439 mts (8,000') is reasonably high. Unfortunately the long slopes above the road keep it hidden. The FGC - Port Ainé ski lift is on the other side of the peak and is a detour in Book 1 of this series.

Villamur is a somewhat larger *pueblo* a couple of miles past Llagunes. Of course it has a bar: the Pic de L'Orri and is on the Coll de Sant Joan 1274 mts (4,179') and more great views of the Siarb valley.

The road now crosses the Serrat de la Cormella del Cortal. The 10 km to Sort does not take long but is very enjoyable. Good tarmac and fast bends. Halfway down, there is another *mirador* if you want to stop and enjoy the great views and clean air.

About 1.5 km before Sort, after a couple of hairpins there is a petrol station if required.

Sort

The word 'sort' is Catalan for "luck". The town is at 692 mts (2,200') (more details in Book 1). In 2017 I stayed in the Hotel Pessets which I liked. It is perhaps fading slightly but comfortable and friendly.

I discovered that during the Second World War many Allied airmen escaping from France were quartered here rather than in the Sort prison where most refugees were imprisoned. There were a number of escape routes that came over the Pyrenees. Franco was clever; he allowed Germany and Italy to use the Spanish Civil War as a training ground for their armed forces but managed to keep them at arm's length. After the War broke out, he trod a precarious path of neutrality hedging his bets by concessions to both sides. Generally, after a few weeks Allied airmen would be repatriated via the Red Cross or American and British Embassies. On the other hand, Jews and other refugees might be sent to Spanish concentration camps or Jews in particular, deported back to Vichy France where the Nazis would be waiting.

The Museu de Cami de la Libertat (road to freedom) is worth a visit if this interests you. They estimate 60-80,000 refugees braved the high mountains, bad weather and the risk of getting caught.

Every year at the beginning of August there is a an event held at the Port de Salau to commemorate the freedom trail and celebrate Occitan identity. Hikers from both sides of the Pyrenees meet at the col which is 2030 mts (6,660') high for a fair. Som Riu at Carrer del Dr. Agustí Muxí i Monroset can arrange a guided tour by 4x4, hiking or horses.

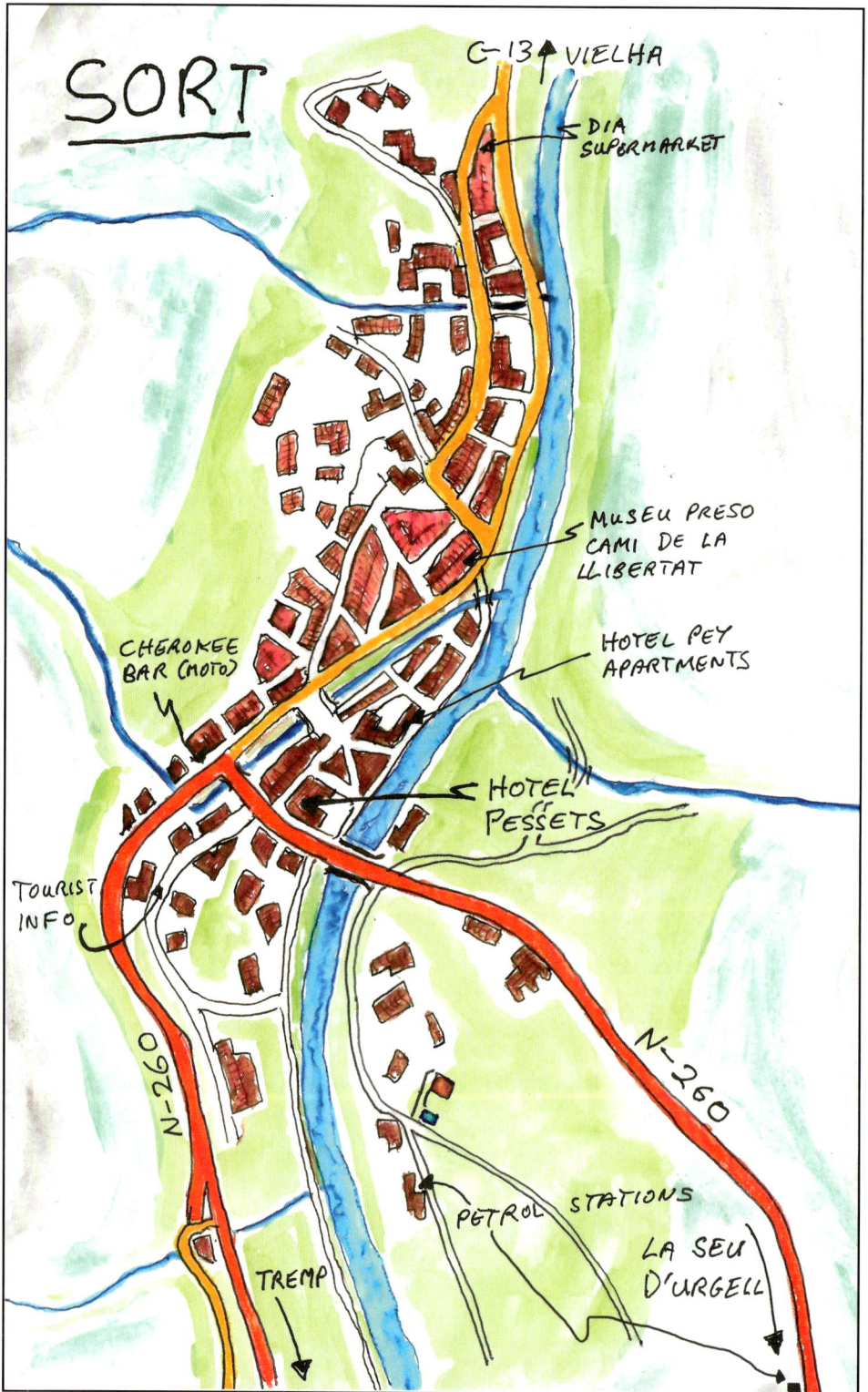

SORT

C-13 VIELHA

DIA SUPERMARKET

MUSEU PRESO
CAMI DE LA
LLIBERTAT

HOTEL PEY
APARTMENTS

CHEROKEE
BAR (MOTO)

HOTEL
PESSETS

TOURIST
INFO

N-260

N-260

TREMP

PETROL STATIONS

LA SEU
D'URGELL

Sort to Vielha - 73 km (45 miles)

Sort is on the Noguera Pallaresa river which joins the Segre just after the Pantà de Camarasa. The Segre flows into the Mediterranean. Era Font d'era Noguereta, the source, is at 2000 mts (6,600') only a 100 metres from the source of the Garonne which flows into the Atlantic at Bordeaux. We are going to follow the Noguera and a subsidiary for nearly 30 miles to the Puerto de la Bonaigua 2072 mts before dropping down to Vielha which is on the Garonne.

The river all the way past Llavorsi is brilliant for white water sports as well as rock climbing and skiing in the winter months.

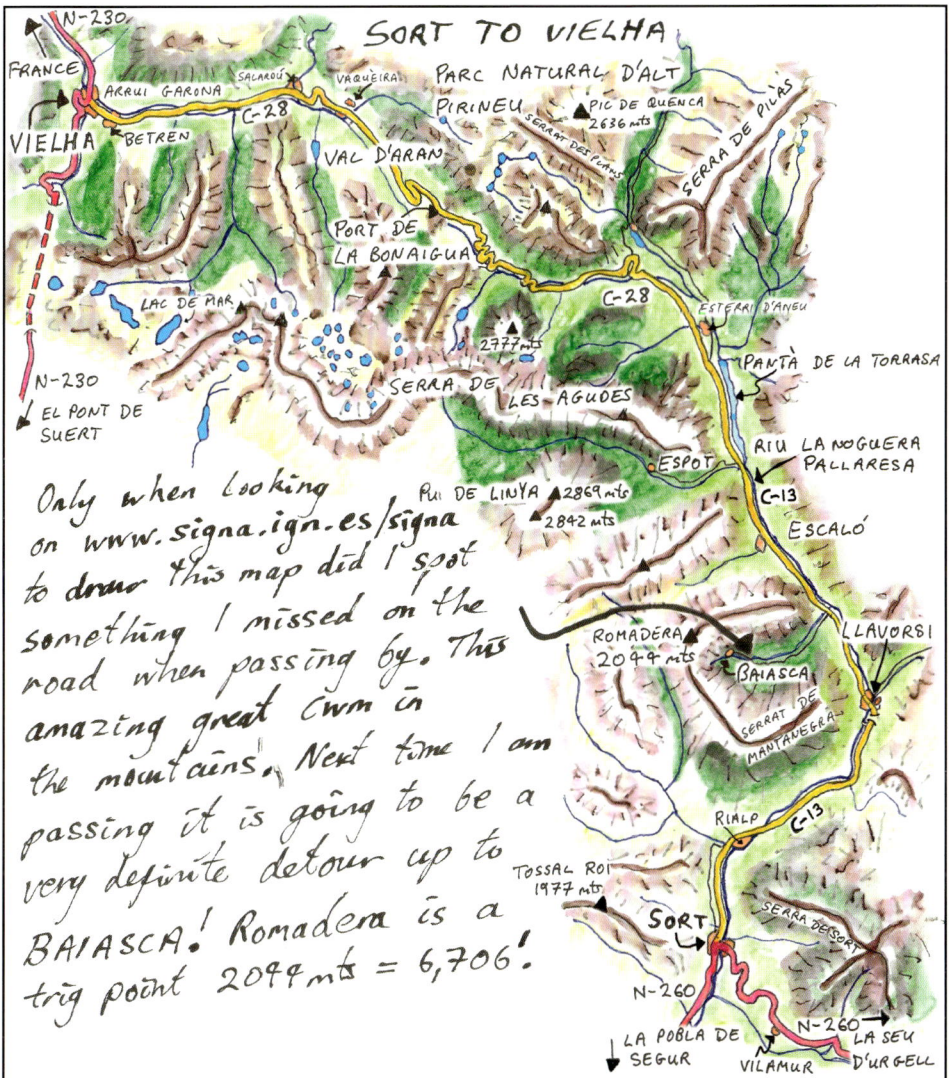

SORT TO VIELHA

Only when looking on www.signa.ign.es/signa to draw this map did I spot something I missed on the road when passing by. This amazing great Cwm in the mountains. Next time I am passing it is going to be a very definite detour up to BAIASCA! Romadera is a trig point 2044 mts = 6,706!

Particularly if in a group it can be worth checking for accommodation in advance in case your visit coincides with an outdoor event. There are a number of campsites and you will find the Camping Noguera Pallaresa 1 km out of Sort on the right-hand side. It looks pleasant and has quite a large 'free' (not plot) camping area but as with others in this popular area it is quite expensive compared to central Spain or Portugal. An adult is €6.20, a tent €6.20, motorcycle €5.80 and car €6.20 (per night). At over €18 for a single person (two in a tent - €25), you might be as well off with somewhere like Hostal Les Collades (around €36) or Hotels like Pessets (€50 - 80). These prices are for May and would be more in high season.

Leaving Sort northward on the C-13 we cruise along the valley bottom next to the river, the steep wooded slopes on the other side rising up in the Serra de Sort and the peak mentioned before: Toretta de L'Orri. At Rialp the valley bends to the north-east and within a couple of kilometres there is the turning for Berani and Roni. This is the detour up to Port Ainé that is detailed in Book 1.

Now the valley narrows with steep and craggy slopes on the left-hand side and more wooded ones on the right. I was struck by the contrast and thought that perhaps the river has exploited a fault line between two types of rock. A little way up here there is a quite large parking bay on the left-hand side of the road which looks an inviting stop; be very careful as it seems to be only available to the oncoming (southward) traffic. There is a SOLID SINGLE CENTRAL WHITE LINE (not to be crossed) and there can be a fair amount of traffic on this main route to Vielha and France.

Around the next corner there is another parking area just above the river where there is not a solid line and so you can, with care, turn across the road onto it.

Further on again you come to the RocRoi Adventure and Rafting Centre (which you can turn into with care) and then just before the short tunnel to Llavorsi the Restaurant Yeti (which you can't).

In 2018 heading north, it was time for a picnic and as I exited the short tunnel I spotted a turn up to the right and took it. It is a pretty rough minor road and around the first bend I found a place to get the bike off the road where it would not be to hard to turn round, the continuing road disappearing round a steep tight hairpin with plenty of gravel. In these situations I have learnt to take the time to investigate on foot before committing to what might become a difficult place to turn the bike (or a car) around. I found a bench looking out over the town and up the valley, slightly marred by electricity wires and pylons but still a pleasant spot for my *pan, chorizo and manchego* (bread, hard cheese and sausage).

Llavorsi is a pleasant little town unfortunately dominated by the hydro-electric plant and all the associated pylons and high tension wires. Plenty of places for a cup of coffee though or a walk by the river.

2019 coming southward I stopped instead just through the tunnel in the Yeti car park, and wandered onto the little bridge.

As I did so a big minibus came to a halt, a woman jumped out and ran onto the bridge with a camera, looking upstream. Her rush was explained as three rubber rafts came sweeping down the tumbling water. The first red one got under the bridge with a slight bump against the rock at the bridge end, the second yellow one got stuck for a short while going round and round in a whirlpool. There was a certain amount of excitement going on. Later, watching the video I had taken, the guides at the back were not making too much effort to avoid the collisions, but it all looked good fun.

Noguera Pallaresa just below Llavorsi

Heading north on the C-13 from Llavorsi we are continuing to follow the Noguera Pallaresa valley; here it is pretty flat in the narrow flood plain between steep hillsides. Long straights take us past Escaló which is pretty small but does have an interesting 11th-century round tower a little above the village.

Further on we come to the Pantà de la Torrassa on the opposite side of which is the Pirineus Parc Aventura with zip wires and tree climbing routes if you need a bit of loosening up.

We are now well into the Vall D'Aneu but in about 4 miles just before Esterri d'Àneu the C-13 turns into the C-28 and past the town we turn up the valley of the Riu de la Bonaigua and the road soon gets more interesting. Here is another little translation prod, *buena agua* in Spanish would be good water so I'm guessing that *bon aigua* is the same in Catalan.

The Val d'Aran near Port de la Bonaigua

Mind you if this river was good water I wonder what was wrong with the Noguera Pallaresa.

A pretty good hairpin lifts us 300' or so into the narrowing Bonaigua valley, the mountains to either side reaching up to the 2,000 mts (6,000') mark. By the time we pass the Hotel Els Avets we are approaching 1500 mts (5,000') and the 10 plus hairpins between 'Km 54' and 'Km 46' (5 miles) are going to get us up to 2072 mts (6,797') at the Port de la Bonaigua. Which is quite high. In fact in early July 2018 I sheltered from a cold driving rain with other bikers in the porch of the closed up Cal del Port restaurant, it was 5°! Unfortunately I had not yet bought my EXOTOGG (see page 80) and despite wearing most of the kit I had with me, got pretty cold. I was glad when I got down into Vielha and found a warm bar.

The Port la Bonaigua is the centre of a web of ski lifts and runs that head up along the crest of the Serra de Cuenques to the north, climbing to nearly 8,500'.

The C-28 crosses a shoulder of mountain that in a long straight and four-stacked hairpins, brings us down into the steeply glaciated valley of the Arriu de Ruda part of the Val d'Aran and the headwaters of the Garonne river (602 km - 357 miles) that, joining with the Gironde, flows into the Atlantic at Bordeaux. So we have just crossed a Pyrenean watershed.

It is only a matter of twenty minutes or so till we are passing through the suburb of Betren and finally entering Vielha. We have dropped down 3,500' to just over 3,000' in under 15 miles.

Parròquia de Sant Miquèu (St Michael's church) Vielha

Vielha

This town is far more complex than one might think. Though it is Spanish and Catalan, geographically it could be French. Massive sierras cut it off from Catalonia, now pierced by the Vielha tunnel on the N-230 which was opened in 1948. Prior to that, the only connection was the high road over the Port de la Bonaigua, often closed by snow in winter. The water here has always flowed into France, and river valleys have been the route of choice down the ages.

The result is that Vielha has a French feel to it and the locals see themselves as different from the rest of Catalonia. In fact they have their own version of the Occitan language (Catalan) - Aranese; it is a mix of Gascon and Catalan and is the third official language of Catalonia. 'Occitania' stretches across southern France and into Italy as well as Monaco though the dialects are under threat everywhere but here. 'Vielha' is Aranese and used on road signs etc instead of the Catalan/Spanish Viella.

I hadn't realised all this but it came up in conversation with the lovely Maria the receptionist of the Hotel Vielha. I always find that a little bit of effort to engage with the people you meet, pays off with insights, as well as information like the best restaurant etc. If a group of you are going to stay in Vielha, then this hotel will very likely do you a special deal. They don't have dedicated parking but you can park on the pavement outside reception which is pretty safe. (See advert on page 79).

Moturisme lists other hotels in Vielha who do have motorcycle dedicated parking including the Hotel Riu Nere but these are smaller and may well be booked up in the season and in fact were full when I asked towards the end of June.

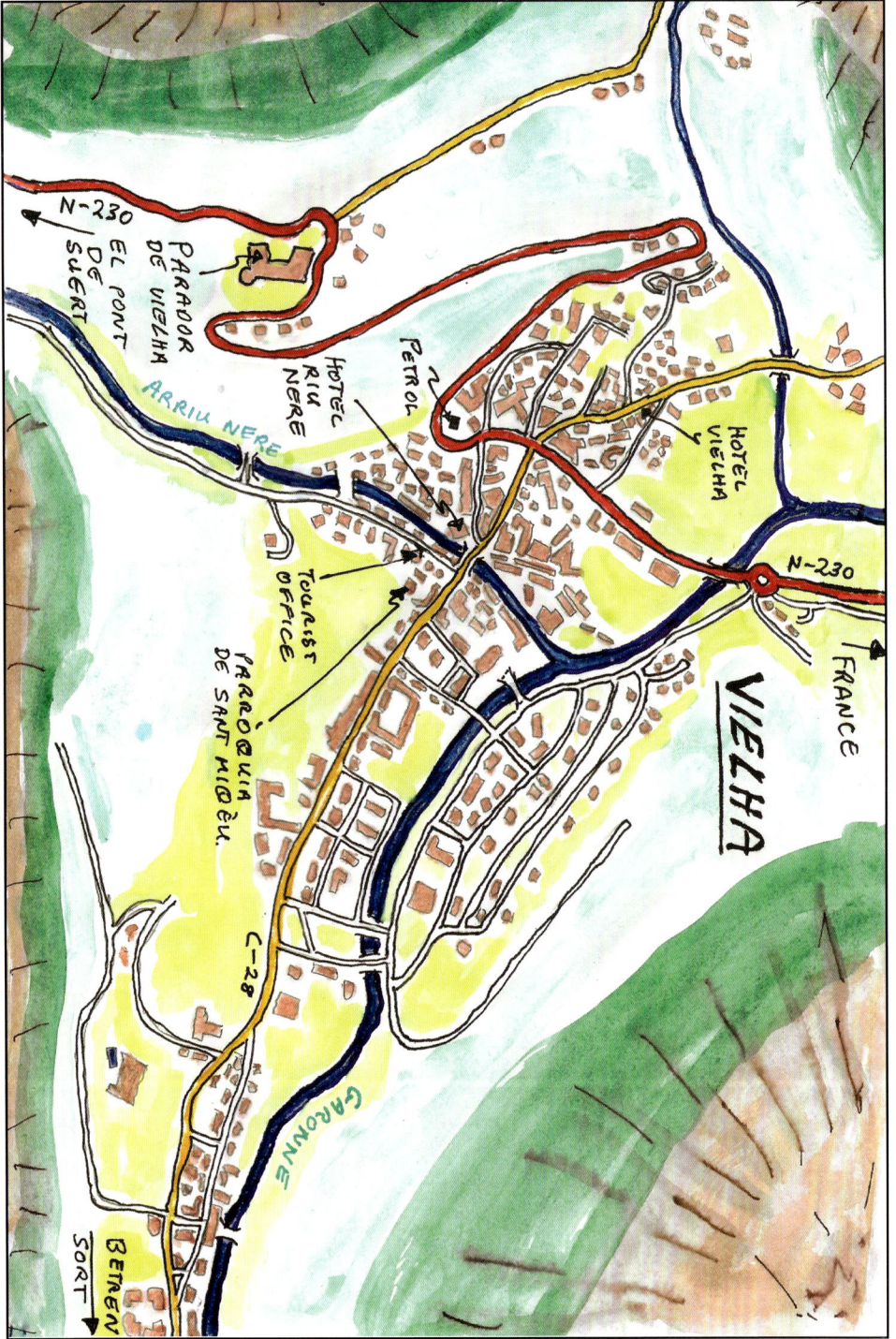

N-230

EL PONT DE SUERT

PARADOR DE VIELHA

ARRIU NERE

HOTEL RIU NERE

PETROL

HOTEL VIELHA

N-230

FRANCE

TOURIST OFFICE

PARRÒQUIA DE SANT MIQÈU

VIELHA

C-28

GARONNE

BETREN

SORT

The town is a busy bustling place, a centre for hiking, climbing, rafting and other mountain pursuits. On my own I tend to get away with just hunting around for somewhere to stay but here as in some of the other towns in the Catalan Pyrenees, the number of visitors can make it difficult and advance booking is probably advisable if you are not as much of a vagrant as myself.

It doesn't take long to get the hang of the town as bang in the middle is a big roundabout: the junction of the N-230 (north to south) and the C-28 (eastward). On the western side of the roundabout is a little *plaça* with the N-230 to Lleida on the left and a minor road on the right. Next clockwise, is the road up to the Hotel Vielha and then the N-230 north to France. Opposite the *plaça* the C-28 is lined with shops bars and the odd hotel until you reach the Plaça Sant Antoni and then the bridge over the Arriu Nere river which tumbles and rushes its way through the town.

Up the little cobbled side streets near the Parròquia de Sant Miquèu (St Michael's church) there are many bars and restaurants. Mountains loom all around.

One of my favourite pastimes is the evening stroll, checking out *menu del dia* prices and occasionally stopping for a coffee and a bit of sketching. The way I travel, I tend to have a couple of *tapas* or a picnic at lunchtime and then enjoy my *vino* quota and a good meal in the evening. The fixed 'menu of the day' is an Iberian tradition. It is worth looking around, as often a matter of a few streets can make all the difference in cost, and what is included. For instance in Barcelona, if you cross the Avinguda Diagonal away from the Passeig de Gràcia and Ramblas, you can halve the *menu del dia* cost.

In 2018 I picked the Restaurant All I Oli. At €19.50 it wasn't the cheapest

but there was a lot of choice and it included wine, water, bread and a desert or coffee (not always included). I particularly liked the look of the *SOPA DE AJO DE LA ABUELA* - Grandma's Garlic Soup for starter and the *CONEJO DE CASA A LA BRASA CON ALL I OLI* - The House Rabbit with aioli cooked on a charcoal grill for main course.

I'm not a fan of deserts but one can always ask for a naranja - orange and you will likely get a naranja preparada 'prepared'.

As often in Iberia the kitchen and cooking is not hidden away where you can't see what goes on. Anyway I had a lovely meal and the owners were very friendly and posed for a photo afterwards. It really takes so little effort;

learning a few basic words and experimenting with them, to make a connection with other human beings.

The wine cooler by the door was an old trough with water in it.

Vielha to El Pont de Suert - 40 km (25 miles)

The last leg of the tour is a pretty straightforward run south to El Pont de Suert; the N-230 takes us all the way, not that it is boring, by any means. Without stopping it will take under 40 minutes.

Heading south from the central roundabout there is a handy Repsol petrol station just before the first of the four hairpins that climb up onto the flank of the Serrat de Pomaròla. The last two bends take us around the Parador de Vielha, a modern building which has great views and would be a nice place to stay if you don't mind being just out of town.

As we gently snake along the mountainside there are spectacular views of craggy peaks walling off the route ahead. These are the Serra de Hont Hereda and others that go up to 2,600 mts (8,500'), and this is what the Tunel de Vielha goes through. The old Alfonso XIII tunnel was the longest in the world when it was opened in 1948 (5.24 km - 3 1/4 miles), and it is now the emergency exit and used by dangerous loads. In winter, the N-230 can easily be closed by snow as the tunnel is at 1,635 mts (5,364').

Take a deep breath and enter the tunnel, just imagine the massive amount of rock above you as dive into the entrance. Popping out the other end you may find yourself in completely different weather, particularly if it was wet or dull in Vielha. We emerge into the impressive 'U-shaped' glaciated valley of the Noguera Ribagorçana. We pass into Aragon before we reach the first reservoir: the Embalse or Embassament de Baserca. There are some parking areas along the *embalse* but the first big one on the waterside is not available heading south so you will have to use one on the right side of the road and carefully nip across the carriageway if you want to go down the water's edge and take photos.

At the dam there is the first of four short tunnels that cut through the obstructing flanks of the Serra d'Evangelis, though by the time we get to Bono the road is running on the flats by the river. Every now and then we stray into and out of Aragon as the border follows the valley. A little after we have passed through the small town of Vilaller, there is another petrol station; this is 30-odd km (20 miles) from Vielha and less than 4 miles from El Pont de Suert. The N-260 from the west joins us just before El Pont de Suert and sets off again southward to El Pobla de Segur.

El Pont de Suert

El Pont de Suert is covered in Book 1 of the series, so I will be brief here.

For accommodation there is the 3-star Hotel Cotori ("unfussy lodging with dining and a terrace") or the cheaper Fonda Isard, both motorcyclist friendly and on *Moturisme's* Accommodation list. There are a number of other hotels in the town, and of course plenty of places to eat and drink.

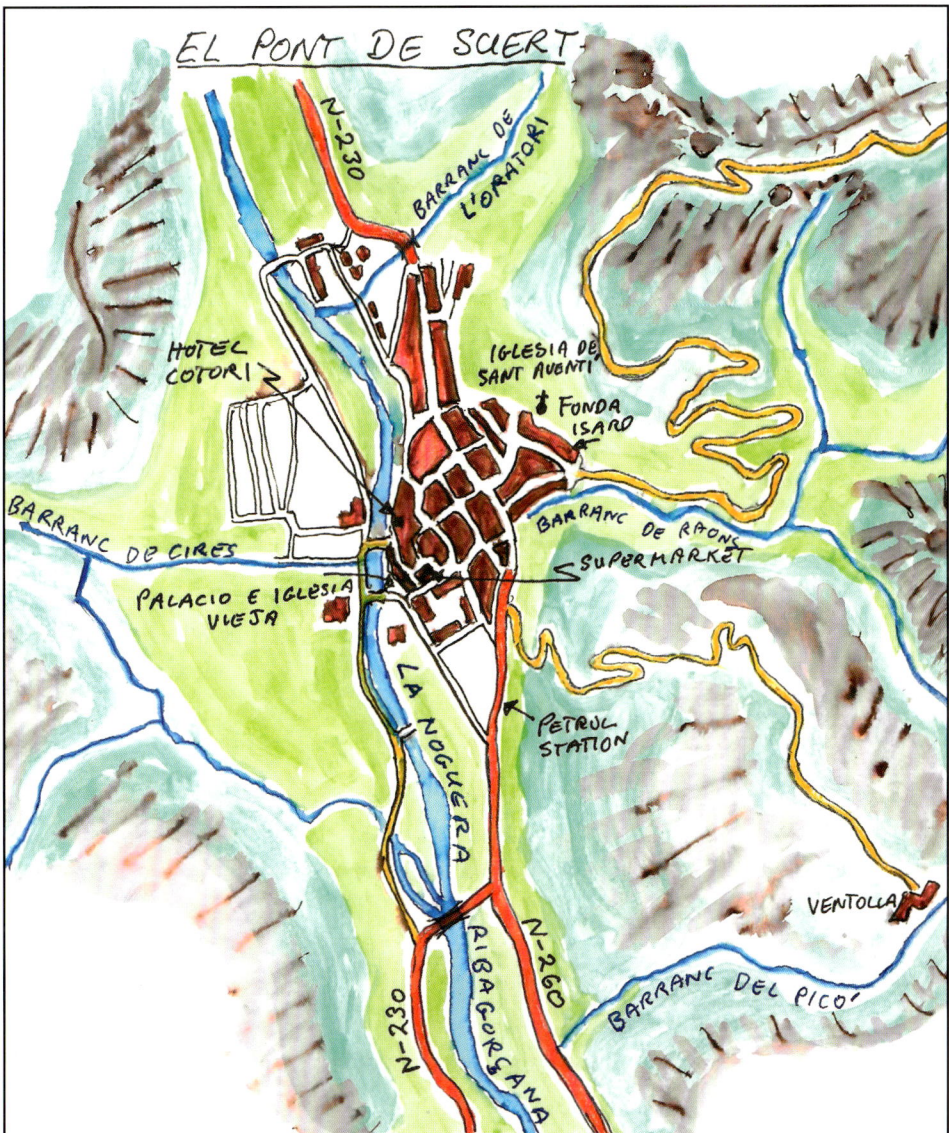

Local fiestas include the Confraria de Sant Sebastiàn towards the end of January (check online for exact dates). It began as a funeral ceremony and now brings together more than 500 men and heads of families, who combine the religious tradition with a celebration of FOOD!

The Fira de la Girella, in October, is an exhibition that focuses on the way of life and old mountain traditions. Locals make and eat the girella, a cured sausage made with lamb's meat and rice, which has been made since the 15th century. The Ball de Bastons is a stick dance (Morris style) which happens at the little village of Malpàs on Sant Pere's day (Saint Peter's, 29th June), and only the men of the village take part.

Centre de Fauna de Pont de Suert (Wildlife Centre), houses otters and European mink and is open throughout the year. There are all types of water sports available at the Escales reservoir and on the Noguera Ribagorçana river.

There is a petrol station as you exit the town southward on the N-230, before the junction with the N-260.

Places of Interest

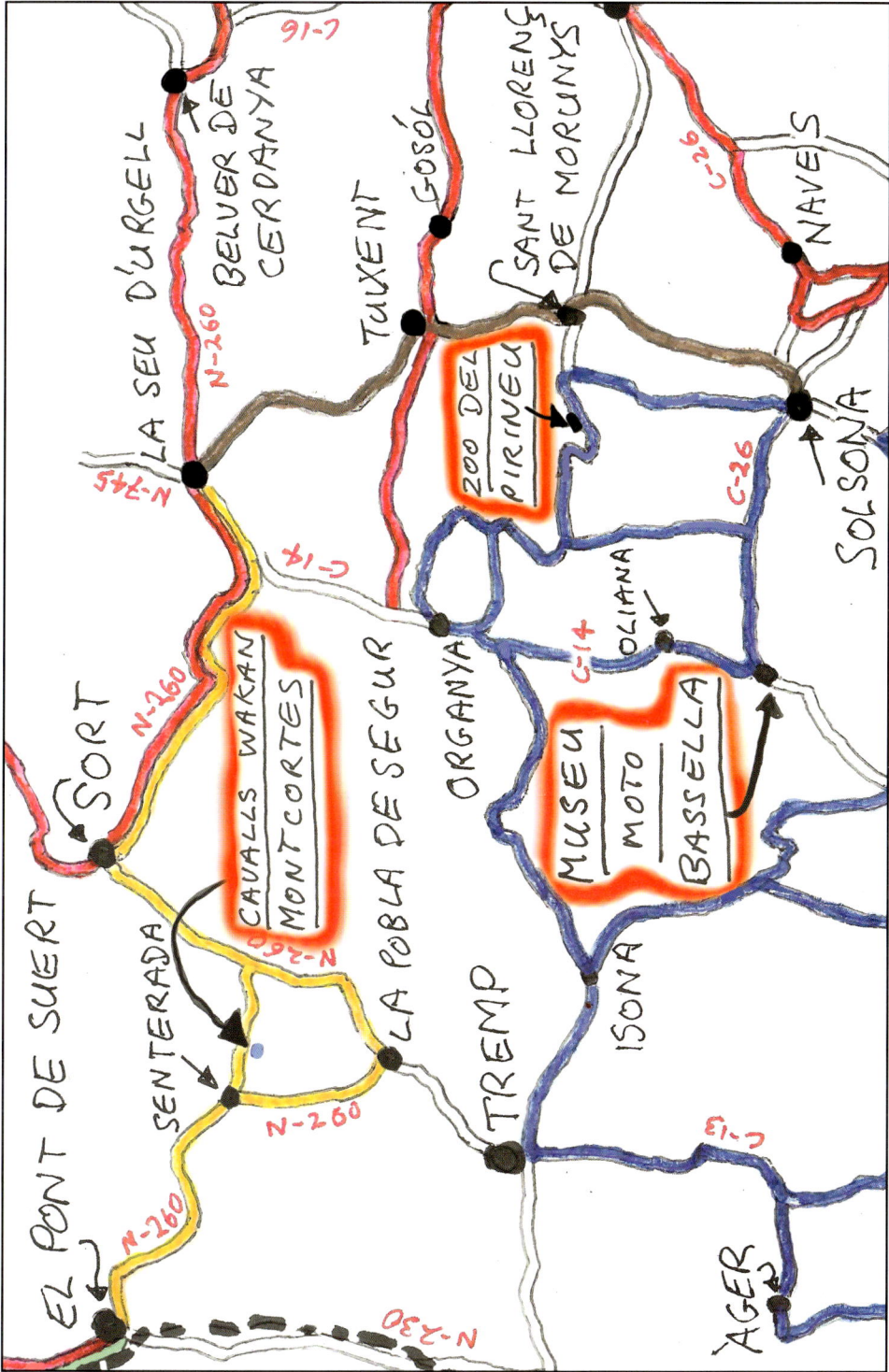

BELVER DE CERDANYA

91-7

SANT LLORENÇ DE MORUNYS

GOSÓL

NAVES

LA SEU D'URGELL

N-260

TUXENT

C-26

N-260

N-345

ZOO DEL PIRINEU

SOLSONA

C-14

C-26

SORT

N-260

CAVALLS WAKAN MONTCORTES

ORGANYA

OLIANA

C-14

MUSEU MOTO BASSELLA

N-260

LA POBLA DE SEGUR

N-260

EL PONT DE SUERT

SENTERADA

N-260

TREMP

ISONA

AGER

C-13

N-260

N-230

Museu Moto Bassella

A fascinating place to visit: covered in detail in Book 3 of the series.

The once-thriving small town of Bassella is now at the bottom of the reservoir Pantà de Rialb. Work started in the 1960s under Franco's regime but there was resistance from the those whose homes, villages and rich agricultural land was going to be inundated. The dam construction only really began in 1992 with the settlements being forcibly evacuated and by 2000, the reservoir was full and the houses and fields all submerged.

In Bassella there was a man (Mario Soler) who loved motorcycles and their restoration. His garage and his bikes were carefully brought to the site of the museum and form the centrepiece of this fascinating experience. Check out all the posters and photos that connect with the era and events of each bike.

Cavalls Wakan & Estanay de Montcortes

A centre for American Quarter Horse treks. They have gentle ponies suitable for any level of experience. Swap your iron horse or box for the real thing. This is Pers' 'learner' horse; she is so forgiving and docile it is like climbing on the sofa! Oh, Pers owns and runs this enterprise, one of those special people to meet, from back street Barcelona to horse whisperer! www.wakan.es

Sketch of Montcortés lake

The Estany de Montcortés nearby is a brilliant jewel of a lake which strangely, is not glacial in origin, but karstic; basically, it is a big sinkhole made by the dissolution of the gypsum rock of the area. It has an underground spring, and is up to 40 mts deep in places with a unique ecology.

Zoo del Pirineu - www.zoopirineu.com

Eagle Owl - 'Duke'

Do visit this amazing place. It is actually an animal rescue centre more than a conventional zoo. The owner Stania and her partner Eloi work immensely hard with very little funding other than ticket sales to keep it going.

Most of the birds of prey of Iberia are represented and it is wonderful to see them close up.

Eagle Owl - 'Duke'

Griffon Vulture

Short-toed Eagle

Feeding the Raven - 'Phineas'

The falconry display is fantastic, having an Eagle Owl brush the top of your head with his wings and sit on your gloved hand with those amazing orange eyes is an unforgettable experience. You will be awed by the speed and dexterity of the Peregrine Falcon coming in to the lure, and amused by the antics of the Little Owl - 'Mr Yoda'.

Peregrine falcon going for the lure and right getting its reward.

There are also many Iberian animals some of which are tame and can be hand-fed and stroked like the Genet and Fox.

It was Stania who explained how the extremely glossy feathers of the raven are important in one of nature's cooperations. Vultures like the Griffon, can suffer badly if they land to scavenge and can't get enough food to replace the energy required to get their heavy bodies airborne again. So ravens will land and check out a sleeping or dead animal; if it is dead they will flap as they try and peck through the skin. The gloss on their plumage reflects and flashes light into the sky where

the vultures will spot it from a long way away and come spiralling in. With their heavy-duty beaks they can rip the animal open and then the ravens will be able to gather up the scraps.

Roadside vulture mayhem

Notes on planning a trip to Iberia

Any vehicle will do as long as you are comfortable with it and plan your journey around it and your capabilities.

WHEN: Iberia and Spain, in particular, is a high mountainous country (avg height 850 mts – 2,788'). From December to April many passes in the Pyrenees and Cordillera Cantabrica can be closed with snow and the north will be frequently very cold, though the south will often be in the mid 20 degrees, or more. In the summer the south can be very hot up to the mid 40's. Most weather systems come in from the Atlantic travelling eastward. The Cordillera Cantabrica and the Pyrenees rising over 6,000' frequently stop the rain from crossing to the south side. This is why the Costa Verde is so green. That weather can also sweep across the Landes in France and keep the French side of the Pyrenees cooler and wetter than the Spanish.

HOW LONG FOR: You can travel big distances on the great roads, but just ticking off miles to destinations is not the way I like to experience the country; get those detours in and plan a realistic and enjoyable trip. I generally don't cruise above 90 kmph - 60 mph and on empty back roads I average only a little less than on a major road. But without speed cameras and the stress of watching your mirror for speeding BMW's or cops. I often travel from around 9 am to perhaps 7 pm taking my time stopping when I like, seeing the country in a relaxed way. Had I been on a motorway or major road I would not be so relaxed and would have done far less hours.

ESSENTIAL KIT: Important documents like MOT, Insurance and vehicle ownership etc. (with photocopies). A UK Driving Licence will quite often be sufficient for ID purposes as it look very similar to an EU Identity Card (you can keep your passport somewhere extra safe). The European Accident Statement Form (downloadable from www. cartraveldocs.com/) is good to have just in case of an accident. A standard form but in different languages.

The EXOTOGG (see page 80) vest packs up very small and is brilliant for those sudden temperature changes that you get in Iberia. July at 6,000 odd-feet on the C-28 to Vielha in the Catalan Pyrenees, it was 5 degrees! No wires so you can use it of an evening when the days' heat has gone and saves on carrying fleeces or extra layers.

Turmeric for grazes or cuts and inflamed mosquito bites. The cooking spice is anti-inflammatory and anti-septic and keeps wounds dry.

An aluminium water bottle kept in a prominent place so that you remember to drink frequently when it is hot and dry. Likewise sun protection.

Motorcycle protective gear. I believe in the benefits of denim (not with abrasion resistance that makes it 'water resistant'). Then with a cotton tee-shirt your hot sweat will be wicked away from your body to keep you cool rather than relying on vents to get air to evaporate it.

Accommodation notes

The Paradors are government-run hotels all over Spain. They are often in marvellous buildings: castles , monasteries and palaces. They are very good value and if you sign up online at www.parador.es as an *amigo* - friend (registration is free), then you can get many special offers, deals and whenever you stay, get points towards a free night.

Hostals are small family-run hotels and away from the worst touristy spots, virtually always decent and reasonably priced. The Spanish love to travel and go out, so a hotel or restaurant with poor service does not generally last very long.

Camping. There a lot of very good campsites, often run by the local municipality and part of the tradition of family holidays in August often to the ancestral area. All will have a good range of facilities.

Be aware that close to Madrid and other big cities, the campsites may be either totally permanent (do not take passers-by) or party sites on the weekends.

Wild camping is generally frowned upon because of the danger of forest fires.

Thanks

My wife and family for putting up with my absences and obsession with researching, writing and producing these books.

Jane MacNamee who continues to add polish to my books by copy-editing, proofreading and culling my commas.

Griselda Sanz Germà, Txell Casas Serena,Carolina Berga and Cristina Soler of Moturisme and Museu Moto Bassella for information and assistance. Nick and Debbie Tunstill of Catalan Adventure for their hospitality.

All my friends in Spain and those who have been my travelling companions.

Raptor identification

BLACK VULTURE

Black Vulture has a 2.9 mts (9.5') wingspan and is the biggest true raptor in the world. Thanks to a reintroduction programme it can be seen in the Pyrenees.

Griffon Vulture. This is the commonest huge bird in the Iberian sky with a massive wingspan of up to 2.7 mts (9').

GRIFFON VULTURE

BEARDED VULTURE

Lämmergeier or **Bearded Vulture** wingspan is almost as big as the Black Vulture but it has narrower wings.

GOLDEN EAGLE

Golden Eagle. 2.3 mts (7.5') wingspan. The **Spanish Imperial Eagle** generally only seen in the Sierra de Gredos and Guadarrama in Central Spain is similar in size and appearance.

BONELLI'S EAGLE

Bonelli's Eagle. Wingspan of 1.8 mts (6').

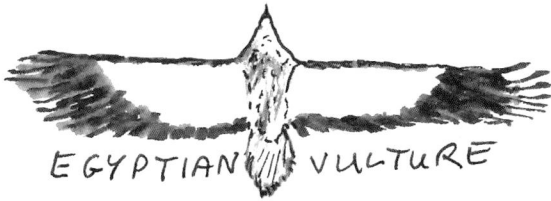

Egyptian Vulture has a wingspan up to 1.7 mts (5.5'). Similar outline to the **Lämmergeier** but smaller. Similar colouring to the **Booted Eagle** but bigger.

EGYPTIAN VULTURE

Short-toed Eagle. Wingspan of 1.9 mts (6.1').

SHORT-TOED EAGLE

Red Kite is familiar to many of us in the UK. Wingspan 1.7 mts (5.5').

RED KITE

Common Buzzard. Wingspan 1.4 mts (4.5'). It is really a small eagle.

BUZZARD

Booted Eagle. With a wingspan of 1.3 mts (4.1').

BOOTED EAGLE

Black Kite is often seen in groups. Up to 1.5 mts (5') wingspan.

BLACK KITE

The **Montagu's Harrier** (summer) and **Hen Harrier** (winter) can often be seen gliding low over fields or open countryside beside the road. **Montagu's** has a 1.16 mts (3.9') wingspan and the **Hen** slightly bigger at 1.22 mts (4.1').

MONTAGU'S OR HEN HARRIER

If you are interested in birds 'Birds of Europe' by Lars Jonsson is still one of the best bird books available.

Books by Duncan Gough

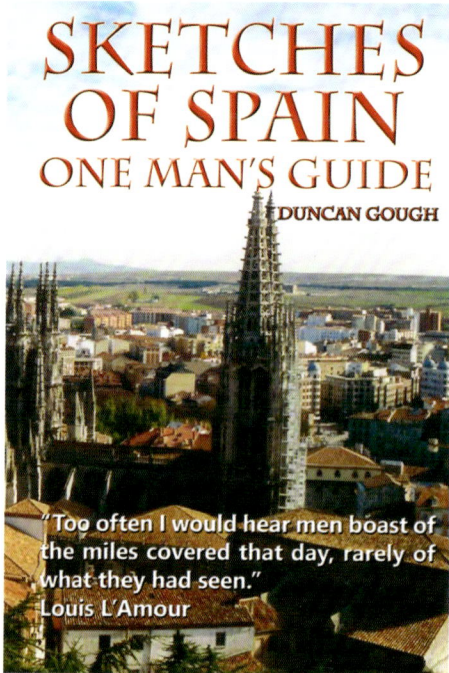

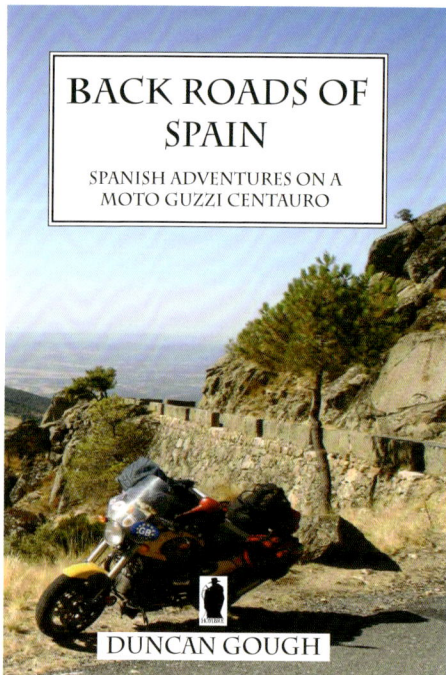

SKETCHES OF SPAIN
ONE MAN'S GUIDE
DUNCAN GOUGH

"Too often I would hear men boast of the miles covered that day, rarely of what they had seen."
Louis L'Amour

BACK ROADS TO MONTE PERDIDO

SANTANDER TO THE PARADOR DE BIELSA

DUNCAN GOUGH

BACK ROADS OF SPAIN

SPANISH ADVENTURES ON A MOTO GUZZI CENTAURO

DUNCAN GOUGH

'Sketches of Spain' is a guidebook covering thousands of kilometres of the back roads of Iberia (Spain and Portugal).

'Back Roads to Monte Perdido' is a detailed guide to an eight-day trip, staying in Paradors on the way to and from the Parador de Bielsa under Monte Perdido.

'Back Roads of Spain' was Duncan's first published book and tells the stories of his first ten years of annual motorbike travels in Spain and Portugal.

All books by Duncan Gough are available from

www.duncan-spanish-travel.com

These Facebook pages may also be of interest:
www.facebook.com/DuncanRGough
www.facebook.com/groups/UKBikersTouringIberia

Other books in the Catalan Pyrenees series

'Back Roads to the Catalan Pyrenees' (0) is a route from the Biscay ports of Santander or Bilbao to El Pont de Suert in Catalonia.

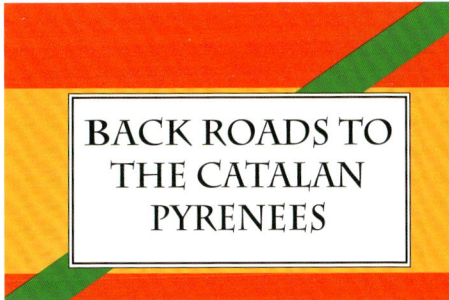

BACK ROADS TO THE CATALAN PYRENEES

BISCAY PORTS TO EL PONT DE SUERT

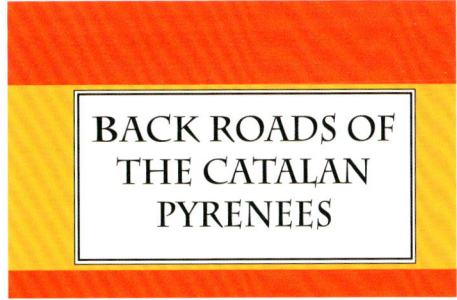

DUNCAN GOUGH

BACK ROADS OF THE CATALAN PYRENEES

EL PONT DE SUERT TO LA SEU D'URGELL

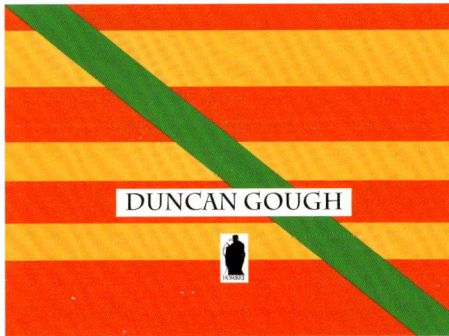

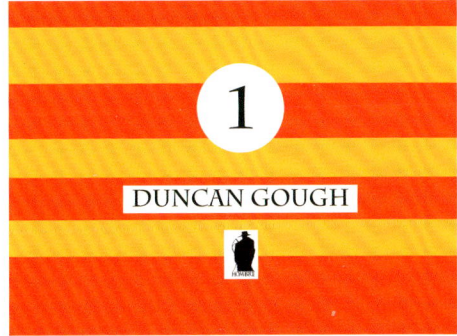

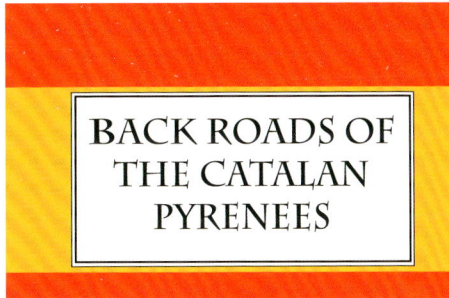

1

DUNCAN GOUGH

BACK ROADS OF THE CATALAN PYRENEES

LA SEU D'URGELL TO SOLSONA

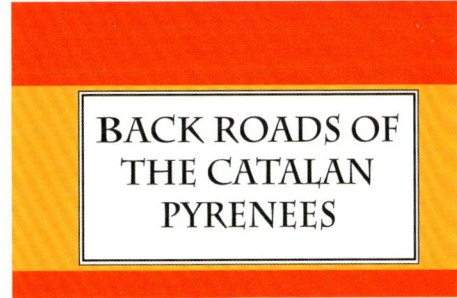

2

DUNCAN GOUGH

BACK ROADS OF THE CATALAN PYRENEES

SOLSONA TO CARDONA

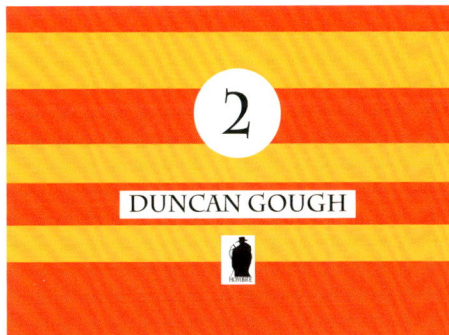

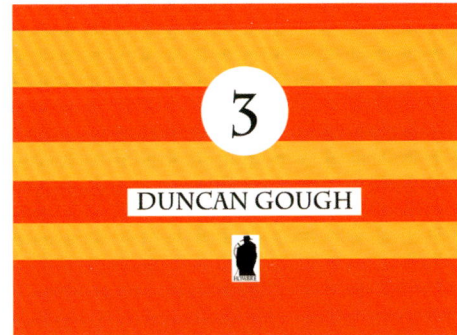

3

DUNCAN GOUGH

The best way to explore France and Spain

Bike Tours in France and Spain available throughout the year

Explore the sights both on and off the beaten track with our pre-planned motorcycle tours to France, Spain and Portugal.

Ride along some of the finest roads in Europe, through magnificent scenery, with so much to discover en route - not to mention sampling delicious local food along the way.

From 3 night getaways to week-long adventures, we've got the right tour for everyone - all you need to do is get on your bike and go!

* Return sailing with your motorcycle
* B&B or Half Board hotel accommodation
* Great choice of pre-planned tours across France, Spain and Portugal

brittanyferries.com/biketouring
0330 159 6716

Brittany Ferries
New horizons, fantastic destinations

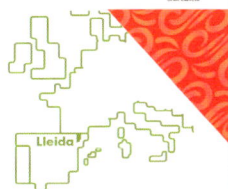

Green Desert Moto Tours are unique!

Each tour is unique because it is designed with reference to the questionnaire that each member of the tour fills out on signing up. No tour is just a repeat. Each day there will be different guided options to personalise the tour even more. Most days groups will ride between 100 and 200 miles but there will also be days that can be spent off the bike enjoying the sights and tastes of places like Sevilla and Burgos or Ávila.

This is an adventure and the emphasis is on the whole experience, not just the great roads and miles covered. It is not just coming back saying "I saw the Alcazar in Seville", it is about who you met, about experiencing local culture and immersing yourself in a foreign country, not just riding through in a bubble.

Duncan Gough will introduce you to his local friends and encourage you to have a go at the language and make your own connections. You will also get bits of history, nature, geography and other knowledge he has picked up in his extensive travels in Iberia.

Hotel in Vielha

HOTEL ★★ VIELLA

Carretera de Gausach 18
25530 - Vielha (LLeida)

973 640 275

www.hotelviella.com

direccion@hotelviella.com

Itinerary Service by Duncan

From information you provide by returning a questionnaire I will create a personal, tailored itinerary to help you get the most from your Iberian tour. Using my extensive knowledge, I will suggest routes, places to visit, things to see and where to stay on a day by day basis.

Enjoy the whole journey, not just the destination. I will give advice on how to avoid motorways and, more importantly, the most dull and boring routes.

I can provide information on Spanish road layouts and legal requirements, if you are unfamiliar with these.

THE COST: £15 for each day of the itinerary. Plus the cost of Michelin maps of the areas covered. For example a 5-day tour (any number of participants) = £75 + maps.

Supplied as highlighted Michelin maps and daily information sheets. NOTE: Not for resale, as the contents remain my copyright.

Contact me through my website below.

www.duncan-spanish-travel.com

Ideal for Iberia where 10 miles can take you up 2,000' and drop the temperature ten or fifteen degrees. Duncan Gough.